THE CONTENT TO CASH BIBLE

Everything You Need to Know to Build
Wealth in the Creator Economy

BY MYQ RODRIGUEZ
W/ ASH CASH

DISCLAIMER

The advice contained in this material might not be suitable for everyone. The authors designed the information to present their opinion about the subject matter. The reader must carefully investigate all aspects of any business decision before committing to him or herself. The authors obtained the information contained herein from sources they believe to be reliable and from their own personal experience, but they neither imply nor intend any guarantee of accuracy. The authors are not in the business of giving legal, accounting, or any other type of professional advice. Should the reader need such advice, he or she must seek services from a competent professional. The authors particularly disclaims any liability, loss, or risk taken by individuals who directly or indirectly act on the information contained herein. The authors believe the advice presented here is sound, but readers cannot hold them responsible for either the actions they take, or the risk taken by individuals who directly or indirectly act on the information contained herein.

Published by 1BrickPublishing
Printed in the United States
Copyright © 2024 by Myq Rodriguez & Ash Cash
ISBN 978-1949303643

DEDICATION

To every creator who dares to turn their passion into purpose, who finds their voice and shares it with the world—this book is for you. And to Coach Glo, aka the Big Plug—thank you for being the catalyst behind this journey. You introduced Myq to Ash Cash and have been a guiding light, mentor, and constant source of inspiration. Your influence continues to shape every page of this book and impacts everyone you connect with. This one's for you.

DEDICATION REQUEST

Please share this book with anyone who you feel would benefit from its guidance, inspiration, and actionable steps for turning their creative passions into lasting success.

Table of Contents

Preface – Introducing Myq & Ash Cash

Your Guides to Creator Success

Thank you for picking up this book. The title tells it all, but since you picked it up, I know that you are ready to take your content and your brand to the next level. Whether you're just starting out or already deep in the game, you're here because you're serious about turning your passion into profit, your creativity into currency, and your influence into income. You're not just looking to create—you're looking to build something that lasts. And that's exactly what this book is about.

Before you dive into the journey of turning your content into cash, it's important to know who's guiding you through this game-changing process. Meet the dynamic duo: Myq Rodriguez and Ash Cash Exantus—two experts with the track record, experience, and insights to help you navigate the creator economy and come out on top.

Who is Myq Rodriguez?

Myq Rodriguez is a powerhouse in the creator economy with a proven track record of helping creators turn their passions into profits. Known for his expertise in media, marketing, and brand strategy, Myq has worked with influencers, digital entrepreneurs, and creatives of all kinds, guiding them from posting content in their bedrooms to landing six-figure brand deals and building globally recognized brands. He's seen the highs and the lows of this industry, and he knows exactly what it takes to succeed. Myq doesn't just talk the talk—he's in the trenches, helping creators every day to navigate the digital landscape and build brands that last. His mission? To make sure no creator is left struggling without a roadmap, armed with the knowledge and tools they need to thrive.

Who is Ash Cash Exantus?

Ash Cash Exantus, widely known as the Hip-Hop Financial Advisor, is a best-selling author, financial educator, and entrepreneur who has dedicated his career to teaching financial literacy and empowering communities to achieve financial freedom. Blending his deep understanding of finance with his love for hip-hop culture, Ash has worked with everyone from emerging influencers to Grammy-winning artists, showing them how to not just make money, but build lasting wealth. With his dynamic approach, Ash breaks down complex financial concepts into actionable steps, helping creatives learn how to manage their money, invest wisely, and turn their talents into sustainable businesses. In the creator economy,

Ash Cash is your go-to for financial strategy and wealth-building—and he's here to ensure you turn your content into a legacy.

Why They're Teaming Up

What started as an introduction from Coach Glo almost 15 years ago has turned into a friendship, brotherhood, and business relationship that took its time to develop. Both Myq and Ash are highly successful in their own rights, but when they reconnected, they realized that combining their expertise would create something powerful. Myq's media and branding genius meets Ash's financial acumen, making them the ultimate team to guide creators in navigating the business side of content creation and maximizing their potential.

Throughout this book, you'll hear from Myq and Ash in a combined voice, sharing their insights, lessons, and strategies. They've written this book together to bring you the best of both worlds—real-world branding strategies from Myq and financial game plans from Ash—to help you elevate your creator journey. So get ready, because you're about to learn from two experts who are committed to seeing you win.

Myq Rodriguez:

What's up, creators? You're about to embark on a journey that's changing lives across the globe. The creator economy isn't just a trend—it's a billion-dollar revolution. As of 2024, the global creator economy is worth a staggering $156.37 billion and is growing at an explosive rate of 22.5% annually. By 2030, it's projected to hit $528.39 billion. That's half a trillion dollars up for grabs! Whether you're posting videos, writing blogs, running a podcast, or building a brand on Instagram, TikTok, or YouTube, you're part of this game. And this game? It's wide open. But here's the thing: if you don't know how to play it right, you're leaving money on the table.

We're here to make sure that doesn't happen. I've seen creators go from posting videos in their bedrooms to signing six-figure brand deals, launching product lines, and building empires. But I've also seen the flip side: talented people struggling because they didn't have the roadmap. That's where this book comes in. We're laying out everything you need to know about the creator economy—from finding your niche to monetizing your influence. We're talking real strategies, no fluff.

Ash Cash:

What's good, family? It's Ash Cash, the Hip-Hop Financial Advisor. And look, Myq hit the nail on the head: this creator economy is the new gold rush. Back in the day, you had to rely on labels, publishers, or big networks to make money off your talent. Now, the power is in your hands. But just like the gold rush, it's not enough to just show up—you've got to have a plan. According to Forbes, there are over 50 million people worldwide who consider themselves creators, but less than 5% of them are making a full-time living off it. Why? Because they don't understand the business side.

This book isn't just about the creative process—it's about getting paid. We'll break down the multiple streams of income that can come from content creation, like brand deals, affiliate marketing, selling your own products, and even creating courses. And we're not just going to tell you what to do; we're going to show you how to do it with real-life examples and step-by-step guides.

Myq Rodriguez:

Let's keep it 100: everyone loves the idea of being a creator, but not everyone's ready for the work that comes with it. It's not just about going viral. It's about building a brand that people trust and that you can monetize. You've got to know your niche, craft engaging content, grow your audience, and most importantly, you've got to manage your money. Too many creators are out here getting big checks, then going broke because they didn't set themselves up right.

When you're building in the creator economy, you're not just a content creator—you're a business. You need to think like an entrepreneur, manage like a CEO, and perform like an artist. And if that sounds like a lot, don't sweat it. We're going to walk you through each step, sharing the mistakes we've seen, the lessons we've learned, and the wins that'll help you level up.

Ash Cash:

Let me tell you something: your content is your currency. But you need to know how to turn that currency into generational wealth.

We're going to talk about finding your niche—because if you're trying to speak to everyone, you're speaking to no one. We'll teach you how to build a brand that's consistent and authentic, and how to create content that not only gets likes but also converts those likes into dollars.

We're diving into the financial side too—because, let's be honest, that's where a lot of creators fall short. From setting up your business structure and understanding taxes to investing in yourself and saving for the future, this book covers the money moves that every creator needs to make. Remember, it's not just about getting to the top; it's about staying there.

Myq Rodriguez:

And let's not forget about the mental game. Being a creator isn't just about the glitz and glamor. You're going to face criticism, trolls, self-doubt, and burnout. But you're also going to have wins, fans, and opportunities that you never thought possible. We'll share how to keep your head right and stay resilient in a space that moves fast and can feel relentless.

Ash Cash:

Look, we're not here to sell you dreams. We're here to give you the tools to make your own. You don't need to be perfect; you just need to be committed. This isn't a get-rich-quick guide. This is a blueprint for building a sustainable and scalable business as a creator. So if you're serious about taking your content from a hobby to a full-blown income stream, you're in the right place. This is your time—let's get it.

Myq Rodriguez:

Ready to take your content to the next level? Let's go. This is more than a book—it's the Content to Cash Bible. It's everything you need to know to build wealth in the creator economy. Like I always say, "I don't chase the bag, I just pick up my luggage." The money is already waiting for you, assigned to you, if you're moving in your creativity and maximizing your full potential. So grab your highlighters, take notes, and let's get to work. The world is waiting for your story—now let's make sure you get paid for it.

INTRODUCTION

Welcome to the world of the creator economy—where your talent, creativity, and hustle meet endless opportunities to build wealth and financial freedom. Whether you're already in the game or just thinking about diving in, this book is going to be your ultimate guide to turning content into cash. We're going to break down the ins and outs of this rapidly growing industry, so you're not just playing the game—you're winning it.

Overview of the Creator Economy

Let's start by talking about what the creator economy actually is. You've probably heard the term thrown around on social media, in the news, or maybe from that one friend who's always trying to go viral. But what does it really mean? At its core, the creator economy is all about individuals—just like you—using digital platforms to monetize their content, skills, and influence. Think of it as a big, wide-open marketplace where your creativity is your currency.

And it's not just about influencers posing with products on Instagram or doing dance challenges on TikTok. We're talking about a multi-billion-dollar industry that includes everything from YouTubers and bloggers to podcasters, OnlyFans creators, digital artists, and even educators running online courses. The creator economy is diverse, and it's evolving fast. According to recent reports, the global creator economy is now worth over $104 billion—and it's only getting bigger.

This new economy isn't just changing how we make money; it's redefining careers. No longer do you need a traditional 9-to-5 or a degree to be successful. Today, your passion, personality, and skills can become your paycheck. And that's why we're here—to make sure you don't miss out on this massive opportunity.

The Rise of Social Media Influencers

Now, let's take a moment to appreciate how we got here. A few years ago, the idea of making money from posting videos or pictures online sounded crazy. "Get a real job," they said. But look at where we are now—social media influencers are everywhere, and they're cashing in big time. From travel vloggers to beauty gurus, fitness coaches to finance educators, influencers have gone from being a niche group of early adopters to mainstream celebrities.

Remember the early days of YouTube, when it was just a place for funny cat videos and grainy home footage? Fast forward to now, and YouTube isn't just an entertainment platform—it's a full-blown career path. Creators like MrBeast, PewDiePie, and Emma Chamberlain aren't just popular; they're multimillionaires with business empires built on the back of their content. It's the same story on Instagram, TikTok, and other platforms where creators are leveraging their personal brands to partner with companies, launch their own products, and even start their own businesses.

The rise of social media influencers has completely flipped the script on marketing and advertising. Companies used to spend millions on TV commercials, hoping people would pay attention during a snack break. Now, they're investing that money directly into creators who can engage audiences more authentically and effectively. Influencers have become the new billboards, but with way more personality and power.

But here's the thing: being an influencer isn't just about taking pretty pictures or making funny videos. It's about building trust with your audience, creating valuable content, and understanding how to turn that influence into income. And it's not just the top 1% who can make a living this way. The beauty of the creator economy is that it's open to anyone who's willing to put in the work.

Purpose and Goals of the Book

Alright, so why this book? Why now? The truth is, the creator economy is still new territory. Sure, there are millions of people creating content, but not everyone knows how to turn that content into cash. That's where we come in. The purpose of this book is to give you the roadmap you need to navigate this space like a pro. We're not just talking about the basics of content creation; we're diving deep into the strategies, the tools, and the mindset you need to build a successful creator business.

Think of this book as your all-access pass to the creator economy. Whether you're looking to become the next big influencer or you just want to make some extra income on the side, we're going to cover everything from finding your niche and growing your audience to monetizing your brand and managing your money. And we're keeping it real—no fluff, no hype, just practical advice that actually works.

One of the main goals of this book is to show you that there's no one-size-fits-all approach to being a creator. Maybe you're into fashion, fitness, finance, or food—whatever it is, there's a space for you. We're going to help you find that space, own it, and turn it into something profitable. But more than that, we want to empower you to think like a business owner, not just a content creator. Because at the end of the day, that's what you are. Your brand is your business, and if you treat it like one, the sky's the limit.

We'll also be breaking down the myths and misconceptions about the creator economy. You might think it's all about going viral, getting brand deals, or having a million followers. But the truth is, you don't need a massive audience to make serious money. What you need is a solid strategy, consistency, and a deep understanding of how to leverage your content. We're going to help you get there.

Another key goal of this book is to prepare you for the ups and downs of the creator journey. It's not all smooth sailing—there will be moments of doubt, times when your content flops, and days when you question if it's all worth it. But if you stay committed, keep learning, and adapt to the changes in the industry, you'll find your way. We'll be sharing stories from successful creators who've been where you are and have built thriving businesses against the odds. Their experiences will inspire you, but more importantly, they'll teach you valuable lessons about what it takes to succeed.

We also want to shine a light on the financial side of being a creator—because let's be real, if you're not making money, it's just a hobby. We're going to break down how to diversify your income streams, manage your finances, and set yourself up for long-term success. From negotiating brand deals and creating digital products to understanding taxes and setting up your business structure, we've got you covered.

And lastly, we're here to remind you that being a creator isn't just about the money. It's about impact, influence, and the freedom to live life on your own terms. It's about connecting with people, sharing your voice, and doing what you love. But if you can make money while doing all of that? Well, that's the dream. And it's a dream that's within your reach.

So, let's get started. Let's turn your passion into profit, your followers into fans, and your content into cash. This is your time to shine in the creator economy, and we're here to help you make it happen. Whether you're starting from scratch or looking to take your existing brand to the next level, this book is your guide. Let's do this.

CHAPTER 1

UNDERSTANDING THE CREATOR ECONOMY

Welcome to the creator economy, where your skills, creativity, and hustle can turn into a thriving business. If you're reading this, you're probably curious about what the creator economy is, how it works, and most importantly, how you can become a part of it. This chapter is going to break down the essentials so you can get a clear understanding of this fast-growing space and why it's more than just a trend—it's a whole new way of working, living, and making money.

Definition and Scope

So, what exactly is the creator economy? Simply put, it's a new marketplace where independent creators—like influencers, YouTubers, podcasters, bloggers, and digital artists—make money directly from their audience. Unlike traditional jobs where you work for a company, the creator economy allows you to be your own boss, using your content as the main product. Think of it like this: if you have a skill, knowledge, or talent that others find valuable, you can monetize it. And that's what sets the creator economy apart from other industries—your creativity is the currency.

Back in the day, if you wanted to share your work with the world, you had to rely on gatekeepers like TV networks, publishers, or record labels. They decided who got to be seen, who got to be heard, and who got paid. But the internet changed all that. Now, with just a smartphone and Wi-Fi, you can reach millions of people without asking for permission. Platforms like YouTube, Instagram, TikTok, and Patreon have democratized content creation, giving anyone with the drive and passion a shot at success.

But let's be real—just because the playing field is more accessible doesn't mean it's easy. The creator economy is a crowded space, and standing out requires strategy, consistency, and a clear understanding of the market. This isn't just about going viral or getting likes; it's about building a sustainable business that can support you long-term. And that's what we're going to dive into in this chapter.

Key Players and Platforms

Now that we know what the creator economy is, let's talk about who's in the game. The key players are, of course, the creators themselves—people like you who are making content and building communities. But there's more to it than just creators. There's an entire ecosystem that includes platforms, brands, agencies, and even the fans who support the creators.

1. Creators At the heart of the creator economy are the creators. These are the individuals or teams who produce content, build audiences, and find ways to monetize their work. Creators come in all shapes and sizes—some focus on education, sharing tips and tutorials on everything from cooking to coding. Others are entertainers, like vloggers and comedians who make us laugh or musicians who share their latest tracks. There are fitness influencers, beauty gurus, gamers, DIY experts, and the list goes on. What they all have in common is that they've figured out how to connect with an audience and deliver content that resonates.

2. Platforms Next up are the platforms. These are the digital spaces where creators distribute their content, engage with their audiences, and often make their money. Each platform has its own vibe and monetization options, which means creators can choose the ones that best fit their style and goals. Let's break down some of the major players:

- **YouTube:** The OG of content platforms, YouTube is a powerhouse for video creators. Whether you're vlogging, teaching, or performing, YouTube offers multiple ways to make money through ads, memberships, super chats, and brand deals. Plus, the long-form video format allows creators to dive deep into topics, build loyal followings, and even expand into merchandise and product lines.

- **Instagram:** What started as a photo-sharing app has evolved into a full-blown marketing machine. Instagram is all about visual storytelling, and its suite of features—from Stories and Reels to Shopping—makes it easy for creators to engage with their audience in real time. Sponsored posts and brand partnerships are big on Instagram, but so are affiliate marketing and selling your own products directly.

- **TikTok:** The newcomer that took the world by storm, TikTok's short-form videos have captivated a whole new generation of creators. It's fast, it's fun, and it's one of the best platforms for going viral. TikTok's Creator Fund and brand partnerships make it possible to earn money, but creators are also leveraging the platform to drive traffic to their other monetizable content.

- **Twitch:** For gamers, Twitch is the go-to platform. It's not just about gaming, though—Twitch also hosts live streams of music, art, and even "just chatting" sessions where creators connect directly with their audience. The monetization options here include subscriptions, donations, and ad revenue.

- **Patreon and Substack:** If you're looking for direct audience support, Patreon and Substack are great options. These platforms allow creators to offer exclusive content to paying subscribers, giving them a steady stream of income that doesn't rely on ads or algorithms.

These are just a few of the many platforms available. The key is finding the ones that align with your content, your audience, and your business model. Remember, you don't have to be everywhere—you just need to be where your audience is.

3. Brands and Agencies Brands play a huge role in the creator economy. They're always looking for ways to reach consumers, and influencers offer a direct line to engaged audiences. This has led to a boom in brand partnerships, sponsored content, and affiliate marketing. For many creators, working with brands can be one of the most lucrative parts of their business, but it's also one of the most complex. Knowing how to pitch yourself, negotiate deals, and deliver value is crucial if you want to make the most of these opportunities.

Agencies are another key player. They help match creators with brands, manage contracts, and sometimes even assist with content strategy. While working with an agency isn't necessary for every creator, it can be helpful once you reach a certain level where managing partnerships becomes overwhelming.

4. Fans and Followers Finally, let's not forget the fans. They're the lifeblood of the creator economy because, without an audience, there's no business. Fans do more than just watch or read content—they support creators through likes, shares, comments, and purchases. Some fans become superfans, joining memberships, buying merch, or even contributing directly through platforms like Patreon. Building a loyal fanbase is about more than just numbers; it's about creating a community that feels connected to you and your content.

Trends and Statistics: How the Landscape is Evolving

The creator economy isn't static; it's constantly evolving. Staying on top of the latest trends and understanding the data behind them can help you stay ahead of the curve. Let's dive into some of the key trends shaping the landscape today.

1. Micro-Influencers and Niche Communities One of the biggest shifts we've seen is the rise of micro-influencers—creators with smaller but highly engaged audiences. Brands have realized that sometimes, less is more. A micro-influencer with 10,000 dedicated followers can drive more sales than a mega-influencer with millions. Why? Because their audiences are often more niche, more trusting, and more connected to the creator.

This trend has opened up the creator economy to people who might not have the biggest following but have a strong voice within their community. So, don't stress if you're not pulling in millions of views. If you're reaching the right people, you're already winning.

2. Diversification of Income Streams Gone are the days when ad revenue was the only way to make money as a creator. Today, diversification is key. Creators are making bank through brand deals, merchandise, digital products, online courses, subscriptions, and more. This not only boosts income but also provides stability. If one income stream slows down, you've got others to keep you afloat.

For example, a fitness influencer might earn money from You-Tube ads, sell personalized workout plans on their website, offer one-on-one coaching sessions, and partner with athletic brands for sponsored content. It's all about finding multiple ways to monetize your expertise.

3. Direct-to-Consumer (DTC) Models Direct-to-consumer sales are booming, especially among creators who want to cut out the middleman and sell directly to their audience. Platforms like Shopify, Etsy, and Gumroad make it easy for creators to launch their own online stores and sell products ranging from digital downloads to physical goods.

DTC isn't just for physical products, either. Creators are selling everything from e-books and courses to exclusive video content. The best part? You get to keep more of the profit, and you maintain control over your brand.

4. The Rise of Live and Interactive Content Another trend that's gaining momentum is live and interactive content. Whether it's a live stream on Twitch, an Instagram Live Q&A, or a Clubhouse discussion, real-time content allows creators to connect with their audience in a more personal and engaging way. It's raw, it's unfiltered, and it's a great way to build deeper relationships with fans.

Live shopping is also on the rise, with creators hosting live product demos and driving instant sales. This trend has been huge in Asia, and it's quickly catching on in other parts of the world. If you're looking to add a new layer of engagement, live content is where it's at.

5. Creator Collaborations and Cross-Promotion Creators are increasingly teaming up to grow their audiences and expand their reach. Collaboration is a win-win: you get exposure to someone else's followers, and they get exposure to yours. Whether it's a joint YouTube video, a guest spot on a podcast, or a co-branded product, working with other creators can open new doors and introduce you to new communities.

Cross-promotion doesn't have to be limited to creators in your niche, either. Sometimes, the best collaborations happen when you mix things up. A food blogger teaming up with a fitness influencer? That's content gold.

6. The Impact of AI and Technology Let's talk about the tech side of things. Artificial intelligence (AI) is transforming content creation, from AI-driven editing tools that make your videos look pro to algorithms that help you understand what your audience wants. There are AI tools that can help with content scheduling, analytics, and even writing. The goal is to make your workflow more efficient so you can spend less time on repetitive tasks and more time creating.

We're also seeing new platforms emerge, each offering unique ways for creators to engage with their audience. The metaverse, NFTs, and other Web3 technologies are starting to make waves, offering creators more ways to monetize their digital presence. While some of these concepts might seem far off, the creators who experiment with new technologies often find themselves ahead of the curve.

The Business of Content Creation

Finally, let's talk business. Because if you're serious about making it as a creator, you need to think like an entrepreneur. Content creation isn't just a passion—it's a profession. And like any business, it comes with planning, strategy, and a whole lot of work.

1. Understanding Your Brand Your brand is more than just your logo or the colors you use on your Instagram feed. It's your voice, your values, and the promise you make to your audience. A strong brand sets you apart from other creators and makes you memorable. Whether you're funny, educational, motivational, or a mix of everything, your brand should be authentic to who you are.

Creating a consistent brand experience across all your platforms is crucial. It helps build trust, which is the foundation of any successful creator business. Remember, people follow people, not just content. They're investing in you, so make sure your brand reflects your true self.

2. Building a Business Model Every successful creator has a business model, even if they don't realize it. Your business model is the way you create, deliver, and capture value. It's how you make money from what you do. Some creators rely on ads, others on direct sales or subscriptions. The best approach is often a mix of multiple models.

Take the time to map out your revenue streams and see how they fit together. Are you making money from YouTube ads? Great. Now, how can you add another stream, like selling a product or offering a service? The more diversified your income, the more stable your business will be.

3. Managing Finances One of the biggest challenges for creators is managing money. When the checks start coming in, it's easy to get caught up in the excitement and forget about taxes, savings, or reinvesting in your business. But if you want to build something sustainable, you need to treat your money wisely.

Start by setting up a separate bank account for your creator business. Track your income and expenses, set aside money for taxes, and don't be afraid to invest back into your business—whether it's upgrading your equipment, hiring an editor, or taking a course to improve your skills. Remember, every dollar you invest in yourself is a step toward your long-term success.

4. Legal and Administrative Essentials Being a creator means you're not just the talent—you're also the CEO, the accountant, and the customer service rep. That means handling contracts, managing invoices, and making sure you're legally protected. Depending on where you are in your journey, you might need to consider setting up a business entity like an LLC, securing trade-marks, or understanding the terms of service on the platforms you use.

You don't need to be an expert, but you do need to educate your-self. And if you can, invest in professional help for the things that are outside your expertise. A good accountant, lawyer, or business manager can save you a lot of headaches down the line.

5. Growing with Your Audience Finally, remember that the creator economy isn't just about one viral moment—it's about growing and evolving with your audience. Trends change, plat-forms change, and audiences' tastes change. The creators who last are the ones who adapt, experiment, and continuously learn.

The business of content creation is exciting, challenging, and full of potential. It's not just about being creative; it's about being strategic. So as you move forward, keep your eyes open for new opportunities, stay true to your brand, and remember that you're building something bigger than just a following—you're build-ing a legacy.

Chapter 2

Finding Your Niche

Alright, creators, let's get real for a second. One of the biggest challenges you're going to face as you step into the creator economy is finding your niche. It's a term that gets thrown around a lot, and for good reason—it's the foundation of your brand, your content, and ultimately, your success. But what does "finding your niche" really mean? And how do you actually do it? Let's break it all down.

Identifying Your Passion and Unique Voice

First things first: if you're going to make it in this space, you need to know what drives you. What's the thing that gets you excited to create, even when you're tired, busy, or just not feeling it? That's where your niche starts—with your passion.

But let's be clear: passion alone isn't enough. You need to find the intersection of what you love, what you're good at, and what people want. So, grab a pen, open up your notes app, or just sit back and think about these questions:

- What topics do you find yourself constantly talking about?
- What skills or knowledge do you have that others find valuable?
- What types of content do you enjoy consuming? Are you a sucker for travel vlogs, cooking tutorials, motivational talks, or DIY hacks?
- What are you naturally good at? Are you the friend who always has the best advice, the funniest stories, or the most stylish outfits?

Your passion is the heart of your niche, but your unique voice is what sets you apart. It's your style, your perspective, and the way you present your content. Think about it like this: two people can talk about the same topic, but how they deliver that information can make all the difference. Your voice is your secret sauce.

Finding Your Unique Voice

Now, finding your voice isn't always easy, especially when you're just starting out. You might feel like you have to mimic other successful creators, but that's the quickest way to lose yourself in the noise. Instead, take inspiration from others, but don't be afraid to let your personality shine through.

Ask yourself: What makes me different? What's my story? Maybe you've been through some challenges that have given you a unique perspective. Or perhaps you have a quirky sense of humor that makes everything you do entertaining. Your voice is already inside you—you just need to let it out.

Here's an exercise: Write down three words that describe you. Maybe it's "funny, bold, and real." Or "motivational, insightful, and down-to-earth." Keep those words in mind every time you create. They're your guideposts to staying authentic.

Another key to finding your voice is to let go of the idea of perfection. No one wants to see a perfect version of you—they want the real, unfiltered version. Don't be afraid to show your flaws, your mistakes, and your journey. People connect with people, not polished personas.

Researching Market Demand: What's Hot and What's Not

Alright, so you've figured out what you love and what makes you unique. Now, let's make sure there's actually a market for it. This is where a lot of creators trip up. They think just because they love something, everyone else will too. But the truth is, you've got to balance passion with practicality.

How to Research Market Demand

Researching market demand doesn't have to be complicated. It's about understanding what your potential audience wants and needs. Here are some steps to get you started:

1. **Start with Google Trends:** Google Trends is like a window into what the world is talking about. Type in your topic and see how it's trending over time. Is interest growing, or is it fading out? Look at related queries and topics to see what's gaining momentum.

2. **Explore Social Media Platforms:** Spend some time on Instagram, TikTok, YouTube, and Pinterest. What kind of content is blowing up in your niche? Look at the hashtags, the popular posts, and the comments. Comments are gold mines because they tell you exactly what people are loving—or hating—about a certain topic.

3. **Check Out Competitors:** Look at other creators in your space. What are they doing well? Where are they falling short? Read the comments on their posts and videos—see what their audience is asking for. This can give you ideas on how to fill gaps in the market or do things differently.

4. **Use Tools Like AnswerThePublic:** AnswerThePublic is an awesome tool that shows you what questions people are asking around your topic. It gives you insight into what's on people's minds, which can help you create content that directly addresses their needs.

5. **Dive into Forums and Communities:** Reddit, Quora, and Facebook Groups are treasure troves of audience insights. Find forums related to your niche and see what people are talking about. What questions keep popping up? What problems are they trying to solve? Use this information to craft content that's highly relevant.

6. **Read Industry Reports and Market Research:** If you're going into a niche that's a bit more professional or technical, read up on the latest reports. Sites like Statista, eMarketer, and even LinkedIn can provide data on trends that are shaping your industry.

What's Hot and What's Not

Let's be real—some niches are more saturated than others. Fitness, beauty, and lifestyle are always hot, but they're also crowded. That doesn't mean you shouldn't go for it, but it does mean you'll need to find your unique angle. On the flip side, niches like sustainable living, mental health advocacy, and niche gaming communities are on the rise and offer opportunities to stand out.

Another tip? Look out for evergreen vs. trending topics. Evergreen content—like "how to save money" or "healthy meal prep"—never goes out of style. Trending topics, like the latest TikTok challenge or celebrity gossip, can drive quick traffic but might not have long-term value. A smart creator balances both to keep their audience engaged and growing.

Differentiating Yourself from Competitors: Standing Out in a Crowded Space

Now that you know what's in demand, it's time to figure out how to set yourself apart. Here's the thing—competition isn't something to be afraid of. It's proof that there's a market for what you're doing. But if you want to thrive, you have to be different. You have to bring something fresh to the table that makes people choose you over everyone else.

Find Your Unique Angle

Let's say you're into fitness. That's awesome, but so are thousands of other creators. What makes you different? Are you the mom juggling workouts with raising kids? Are you focused on fitness for beginners who've never stepped foot in a gym? Or maybe you're all about mental health and fitness, focusing on how working out can be a form of therapy. That's your angle.

Your angle isn't just about your content—it's about your story. People connect with stories, not just information. Think about it: why do you watch certain creators over others? It's usually because their story resonates with you in some way. Maybe they've overcome something you're struggling with, or they represent a version of yourself that you aspire to be.

Be Consistently You

Consistency is one of the most underrated aspects of differentiation. If you're known for your witty, sarcastic takes on pop culture, don't suddenly switch to being super serious just because you think it might attract a different audience. Your audience shows up for you, not just the topic. The more consistently you show up as yourself, the more people will recognize your brand—and that's what keeps them coming back.

Leverage Your Strengths

Think about your strengths. Are you great at storytelling? Lean into that with longer videos or narrative-driven content. Are you a killer photographer? Make your visuals pop in a way that no one else can. Don't try to be everything—focus on what you do best and make that your signature.

Create Value

Standing out isn't just about being different; it's about providing value that others aren't. Are you solving a problem? Are you teaching something new? Are you offering a fresh perspective? Every piece of content you put out should answer the question, "What's in it for the viewer?" Whether it's entertainment, education, or inspiration, make sure you're giving something valuable in every post.

Engage Like No One Else

One of the best ways to differentiate yourself is by engaging with your audience on a deeper level. Reply to comments, ask for feedback, and show that you actually care about your community. People love to feel seen and heard, and when you take the time to engage, it sets you apart from the creators who just post and ghost.

Create Signature Content Series

Another strategy is to create a signature content series—something that's uniquely yours. Think of it like a recurring segment that people can look forward to. Maybe it's a weekly Q&A, a themed tutorial, or a fun challenge you run with your followers. Signature series not only create anticipation but also make your content more recognizable.

Testing Your Ideas Before Going All In

So you've identified your passion, found your unique voice, researched your market, and figured out how you'll stand out. But before you dive in headfirst, there's one more crucial step: testing your ideas. Testing helps you validate your concept, refine your approach, and ensure there's an audience ready for what you're offering.

Start Small

One of the best ways to test your niche is to start small. You don't need to quit your day job or invest a ton of money upfront. Begin by creating a few pieces of content that reflect your niche and see how they perform. If you're thinking about starting a YouTube channel, post a few videos. If Instagram is your thing, create a series of posts or Reels that showcase your angle.

Pay attention to the response. Are people engaging? Are they asking for more? Don't be discouraged if things don't blow up immediately—remember, growth takes time. But if you're getting good feedback, that's a strong sign you're on the right track.

Use Polls and Surveys

Your audience is one of your best resources for feedback. Use Instagram polls, Twitter surveys, or even a simple post asking what kind of content they want to see. This not only gives you valuable insights but also makes your audience feel involved in your process.

A/B Test Your Content

If you're not sure what style, format, or angle works best, try A/B testing. Post similar content in different styles or with different approaches, and see which one gets better engagement. Maybe you try a funny video and a more serious one on the same topic. Or you compare a long-form article with a quick tip post. A/B testing allows you to gather data and make informed decisions about what resonates most with your audience.

Experiment with Different Platforms

Not every niche performs the same on every platform. You might find that your style of content works better on TikTok than on YouTube, or that your niche is more popular on Pinterest than Instagram. Don't be afraid to experiment with different platforms to see where your content gets the most traction.

Analyze the Data

After testing, dive into your analytics. What's working? What's not? Look beyond the vanity metrics of likes and views—focus on meaningful engagement. Are people commenting, sharing, and saving your posts? Are they clicking through to your website or signing up for your newsletter? Use this data to refine your approach and double down on what's working.

Be Willing to Pivot

Testing might reveal that your original idea isn't landing the way you hoped. That's okay. Pivoting isn't failure—it's part of the process. Be willing to adjust your content, shift your focus, or even change your niche altogether if the data tells you that's the best move. The creator economy is all about flexibility and staying in tune with your audience's needs.

Stay True to Your Vision

Finally, remember that testing is about finding the sweet spot between what you love and what your audience loves. Don't get so caught up in what the numbers say that you lose sight of why you started. Your niche should be something you're excited about—a space where you can thrive creatively and connect with others.

The journey to finding your niche isn't always straightforward, but it's one of the most important steps you'll take as a creator. It sets the stage for everything else you'll build. So take your time, do your research, test your ideas, and above all, stay true to yourself. Your niche is out there, waiting for you to claim it. Now go get it.

CHAPTER 3

BUILDING YOUR BRAND

Alright, creators, now that you've found your niche, it's time to talk about one of the most important elements of your journey: building your brand. Your brand is more than just your logo, your color scheme, or the fonts you use on your website. It's the entire experience that people have with you, your content, and your business. It's how you tell your story, how you connect with your audience, and how you stand out in a sea of creators. Think of your brand as your signature—it's what makes you uniquely you, and it's what keeps people coming back for more.

Crafting a Unique Personal Brand: Storytelling and Authenticity

Let's start by breaking down what it means to craft a unique personal brand. Your brand isn't just about what you do; it's about who you are. It's your personality, your values, your voice, and your story all wrapped into one. And let's be real—people don't just follow brands; they follow people. They connect with the humans behind the content, the ones who are real, relatable, and authentic.

The Power of Storytelling

One of the most powerful tools you have as a creator is storytelling. Humans are wired to connect through stories. It's how we've communicated for centuries, and it's what makes us feel something. Think about the creators you love—chances are, it's not just their content you're drawn to; it's their story. Maybe they've overcome adversity, maybe they've achieved something you aspire to, or maybe they just make you laugh when you need it most.

Your story doesn't have to be some grand, life-changing tale. It just needs to be yours. So, what's your story? How did you get started? What challenges have you faced? What are you passionate about? These are the questions that will help you craft a narrative that resonates with your audience.

Authenticity Is Your Superpower

We hear the word "authenticity" a lot, but what does it really mean? Being authentic doesn't mean you have to share every detail of your life or always be vulnerable. It means being true to who you are, even when it's not perfect. It's about showing up as yourself, flaws and all, and not pretending to be something you're not.

Authenticity is powerful because it builds trust, and trust is the foundation of any successful brand. When you're authentic, people feel it. They can tell when you're being real, and they can also tell when you're putting on a show. So, embrace your quirks, your mistakes, and your unique perspective. That's what makes you, you.

Finding Your Brand Voice

Your brand voice is how you communicate with your audience—it's the words you use, the tone you take, and the way you make people feel when they interact with your content. Are you funny and sarcastic? Are you motivational and uplifting? Are you direct and no-nonsense? Your voice should be a reflection of your personality.

To find your voice, think about how you naturally speak to your friends or family. How would you explain your niche to someone who knows nothing about it? Your voice doesn't have to be formal or polished; it just needs to be consistent and true to you.

Developing a Strong Online Presence: The Do's and Don'ts

Now that you've got a handle on your brand's story and voice, let's talk about developing a strong online presence. Your online presence is like your digital storefront—it's where people go to learn more about you, your brand, and what you have to offer. And just like a physical store, first impressions matter.

The Do's of Building Your Online Presence

- **Do Be Consistent Across Platforms:** Consistency is key when it comes to your brand. Your username, profile picture, bio, and overall vibe should be similar across all platforms. This doesn't mean you have to post the exact same content everywhere, but your brand should feel cohesive no matter where people find you.

- **Do Optimize Your Bio and About Section:** Your bio is one of the first things people see, so make it count. Be clear about who you are, what you do, and why people should follow you. Use keywords that reflect your niche and make it easy for people to understand what you're all about.

- **Do Invest in Quality Visuals:** Visuals are a huge part of your brand's identity. You don't need to be a professional photographer or graphic designer, but investing in quality visuals—whether that's photos, videos, or graphics—can make a big difference. High-quality content shows that you take your brand seriously and helps you stand out.

- **Do Engage with Your Audience:** Building an online presence isn't just about posting content; it's about creating a community. Engage with your followers by responding to comments, asking questions, and showing appreciation. Engagement isn't just a metric—it's how you build relationships.

- **Do Have a Content Strategy:** Posting randomly without a plan can lead to inconsistent results. Create a content strategy that outlines what you'll post, when you'll post, and why it matters to your audience. This will keep you on track and ensure that your content aligns with your brand's goals.

- **Do Showcase Your Personality:** Your online presence shouldn't feel like a stiff, corporate brand. Show your personality, share behind-the-scenes moments, and let people see the real you. Whether it's through Instagram Stories, TikTok videos, or Twitter threads, find ways to let your audience in.

The Don'ts of Building Your Online Presence

1. **Don't Be Everything to Everyone:** One of the biggest mistakes creators make is trying to appeal to everyone. Your brand isn't for everyone, and that's okay. Focus on your target audience—the people who resonate with your message—and don't worry about pleasing the rest.

2. **Don't Post Inconsistently:** Inconsistent posting can make your brand feel unreliable. It's okay to take breaks when needed, but try to stick to a schedule that works for you. Consistency builds trust, and it keeps you top-of-mind for your audience.

3. **Don't Ignore Your Analytics:** Analytics are your best friend when it comes to understanding what's working and what's not. Pay attention to your data—like which posts get the most engagement, what times your audience is online, and what content types perform best. Use this information to refine your strategy.

4. **Don't Get Stuck in Comparison Mode:** It's easy to fall into the trap of comparing yourself to other creators, but it's a surefire way to kill your motivation. Remember, everyone's journey is different. Focus on your path, your growth, and your unique strengths.

5. **Don't Over-Promise and Under-Deliver:** Be mindful of what you promise your audience. If you say you're going to do something—whether it's a product launch, a video series, or a collaboration—make sure you follow through. Consistency in your actions builds credibility.

6. **Don't Forget to Be Human:** At the end of the day, social media is about connecting with other humans. Don't be afraid to show your flaws, admit when you don't have all the answers, or share a personal story. The more relatable you are, the more your audience will connect with you.

Consistency is Key: Creating a Memorable Brand Identity

Let's talk about the magic word: consistency. Consistency is what turns your brand from a one-hit wonder into something memorable and reliable. It's what makes your audience think of you first when they need what you offer. And it's the difference between a brand that fades into the background and one that stands out.

Consistency in Content

One of the most important aspects of consistency is your content. That doesn't mean you have to post every day or be on every platform, but it does mean showing up regularly and delivering the kind of content your audience expects from you. Consistent content helps your audience know what to expect, and it builds a sense of familiarity and trust.

Whether it's weekly YouTube videos, daily Instagram posts, or a monthly newsletter, find a schedule that works for you and stick to it. If you ever need to take a break or change your posting frequency, just communicate that with your audience. They'll appreciate your honesty, and it keeps the trust intact.

Consistency in Visuals

Your visuals are a huge part of your brand identity, and consistency here can make you instantly recognizable. This includes your color scheme, fonts, photo style, and overall aesthetic. Think of it like the visual language of your brand—it should feel cohesive across all your platforms.

For example, if your brand colors are blue and gold, try to incorporate those into your graphics, thumbnails, and even your wardrobe if it fits. If your photos have a bright and airy vibe, keep that style consistent. Your visuals should feel like a natural extension of your brand's personality.

Consistency in Messaging

Your messaging is how you communicate your brand's values, mission, and personality. It's the words you use in your captions, your website copy, and even your interactions with your audience. Consistent messaging helps reinforce your brand's identity and makes your audience feel like they know you.

For example, if your brand is all about positivity and motivation, your messaging should reflect that. Your tone should be encouraging, your language should be uplifting, and your content should inspire. Consistency in messaging isn't just about the words you choose—it's about the overall feeling you create.

Consistency in Engagement

Engagement is another area where consistency is key. Your audience wants to feel connected to you, and that connection is built over time through consistent interactions. Respond to comments, answer questions, and engage with your community regularly. Even small interactions can go a long way in building a loyal fanbase.

Consistency Builds Trust

At the core of consistency is trust. When people see that you show up regularly, that your brand is reliable, and that your message is clear, they're more likely to trust you. And trust is what leads to deeper connections, loyal followers, and ultimately, brand success.

Leveraging Emotional Marketing to Connect with Your Audience

Last but definitely not least, let's dive into the power of emotional marketing. Emotional marketing is all about connecting with your audience on a deeper level by tapping into their feelings, desires, and values. It's not just about selling a product or promoting a video—it's about creating an emotional experience that makes your audience feel seen, understood, and inspired.

Know Your Audience's Pain Points

One of the most effective ways to connect emotionally is by addressing your audience's pain points. What are they struggling with? What keeps them up at night? What problems are they trying to solve? When you create content that speaks directly to these pain points, your audience feels like you get them—and that's a powerful connection.

For example, if you're in the wellness space, your audience might be dealing with stress, burnout, or body image issues. Your content should address these challenges with empathy, offering solutions, support, and encouragement. It's about showing that you're not just here to talk at them—you're here to help them.

Use Storytelling to Evoke Emotion

We've already touched on the importance of storytelling, but it's worth repeating—stories are one of the most powerful tools you have. Stories evoke emotion because they're relatable, personal, and memorable. Whether you're sharing your own experiences, highlighting a customer testimonial, or creating a narrative around your brand, storytelling allows you to connect on a human level.

When crafting your stories, think about the emotions you want to evoke. Do you want your audience to feel inspired? Empowered? Motivated to take action? Use your stories to guide your audience on an emotional journey that aligns with your brand's message.

Create Content That Resonates with Your Audience's Values

Another way to leverage emotional marketing is by aligning your content with your audience's values. People are drawn to brands that reflect their own beliefs and ideals, so think about what values your brand represents. Is it authenticity, creativity, empowerment, sustainability, or something else? Incorporate those values into your content to create a deeper connection.

For example, if sustainability is a core value of your brand, showcase the ways you incorporate eco-friendly practices into your life or business. Share tips, products, or resources that help your audience live more sustainably. When your content aligns with your audience's values, it resonates on a much deeper level.

Use Visuals and Music to Set the Tone

Emotions aren't just conveyed through words—they're also communicated through visuals and music. The colors you choose, the style of your videos, and the music you use all play a role in setting the emotional tone of your content. If you want your audience to feel calm and relaxed, opt for soft colors and soothing music. If you want them to feel energized and excited, go for bold visuals and upbeat tunes.

Don't underestimate the power of aesthetics in creating an emotional experience. Your visuals and music should be an extension of your brand's personality and the feelings you want to evoke in your audience.

Show Vulnerability

One of the most powerful ways to connect with your audience is by showing vulnerability. Sharing your struggles, failures, and lessons learned humanizes you and makes you relatable. It's not about airing all your dirty laundry, but about letting your audience see that you're not perfect—and that's okay.

When you show vulnerability, you create a safe space for your audience to be vulnerable too. They see that they're not alone in their challenges, and that builds a strong emotional bond. So don't be afraid to share the real moments, the tough times, and the behind-the-scenes of your journey. It's those moments that make your brand feel genuine and relatable.

Inspire Action Through Emotion

Finally, emotional marketing isn't just about making your audience feel something—it's about inspiring them to take action. Whether it's subscribing to your channel, purchasing your product, or simply sharing your content, use emotion to motivate your audience to do something meaningful.

Call-to-actions (CTAs) that tap into emotion are often more effective than generic ones. Instead of just saying "subscribe now," try something like "join our community and start your journey to success today." Make your audience feel like they're part of something bigger, and they'll be more likely to take that next step.

Building your brand is a journey, but it's one of the most rewarding parts of being a creator. It's your chance to share your story, connect with people, and create something that's uniquely yours. By crafting a personal brand that's authentic, consistent, and emotionally resonant, you're not just building a brand—you're building a legacy. So lean into your story, let your personality shine, and create a brand that truly reflects who you are.

Now, let's go build something amazing.

CHAPTER 4

CREATING ENGAGING CONTENT

Alright, creators, let's get down to business—creating content that not only looks good but also grabs attention, holds it, and keeps people coming back for more. You've got your niche, you've built your brand, and now it's time to put it all into action with content that speaks to your audience in a way that feels authentic and compelling. This chapter is all about taking your ideas from your brain to the screen, and we're going to walk through it together, step by step.

Creating engaging content isn't just about slapping together a few clips or writing a quick post. It's about planning, execution, and constantly refining your approach. Whether you're creating videos, podcasts, blogs, or social media posts, your content is your way of connecting with your audience, telling your story, and sharing your expertise. So, let's dive in and break down how to make content that doesn't just get views—it makes an impact.

Content Creation Strategies: From Planning to Execution

If you want your content to be successful, you can't just wing it. Sure, some of the best ideas come from spontaneous moments, but if you want to create consistently engaging content, you need a strategy. This means knowing what you're going to create, why you're creating it, and how it fits into your overall brand.

1. Start with Your Goals

Before you start creating, you need to get clear on your goals. What do you want your content to achieve? Are you trying to grow your audience, drive traffic to your website, sell a product, or build brand awareness? Your goals will shape the type of content you create and how you present it.

For example, if your goal is to educate your audience, you might create tutorial videos, how-to guides, or infographics. If your goal is to entertain, you might focus on vlogs, skits, or challenges. And if you're trying to sell something, your content might include product demos, testimonials, or promotional posts.

2. Know Your Audience

One of the biggest mistakes creators make is creating content for themselves, not their audience. Yes, it's your brand, but it's your audience who consumes your content. Take the time to understand who they are, what they like, and what they're struggling with. Use analytics, polls, comments, and direct feedback to gather insights into what resonates most with them.

Imagine your ideal audience member: What are their interests? What problems do they need solved? What type of content do they enjoy? When you create with your audience in mind, your content will be more relevant, engaging, and valuable.

3. Create a Content Calendar

Consistency is key, and the best way to stay consistent is by planning ahead with a content calendar. A content calendar helps you organize your ideas, set deadlines, and ensure you're delivering content regularly. It doesn't have to be anything fancy—you can use a simple spreadsheet, a Google Calendar, or a project management tool like Trello or Asana.

Here's how to get started:

- **Brainstorm Content Ideas:** Set aside time each month to brainstorm content ideas. Think about what's trending, what questions your audience is asking, and what themes align with your brand's message.
- **Plan Your Content Types:** Decide what type of content you'll create—videos, blogs, podcasts, social media posts— and how often you'll publish each one.
- **Set Deadlines:** Assign deadlines for each piece of content, including planning, creation, and publishing dates. This will keep you on track and prevent last-minute scrambling.

- **Mix It Up:** Keep your content calendar varied by including different types of content—educational, entertaining, inspirational, promotional, etc. This keeps your audience engaged and prevents your content from feeling repetitive.

4. Outline Your Content

Once you've planned what you're going to create, it's time to outline your content. Outlining helps you organize your thoughts, ensure you cover all the important points, and stay focused on your message. This is especially important for longer content like videos, podcasts, or blog posts.

For example, if you're creating a YouTube video, your outline might include an introduction, key talking points, visuals or props needed, and a call-to-action. If you're writing a blog post, your outline might break down the main sections, subheadings, and key takeaways.

Outlining doesn't mean scripting everything word for word (unless that's your style); it's just a roadmap to keep you on track. The more organized your content, the easier it will be to create and the better it will flow for your audience.

5. Batch Your Content Creation

If you want to save time and stay consistent, batching is your best friend. Batching means creating multiple pieces of content in one sitting instead of doing everything one at a time. For example, instead of filming one video every week, set aside a day to film four videos back-to-back. Or if you're writing blog posts, draft several at once and schedule them to be published over time.

Batching not only streamlines your workflow but also helps you get into a creative groove. You'll spend less time setting up and more time actually creating. Plus, having content ready in advance means you're never scrambling to get something out at the last minute.

6. Execution: Bringing Your Content to Life

Now that you've planned and prepped, it's time for the fun part—execution. When it's time to create, set the stage for success. Make sure you're in a good headspace, free of distractions, and ready to bring your ideas to life.

Focus on quality, but don't get hung up on perfection. The creator economy moves fast, and sometimes it's better to put out good content consistently than to wait until everything is perfect. Done is better than perfect, and every piece of content is a chance to learn, improve, and connect with your audience.

Storytelling Techniques: How to Make Your Content Captivating

Storytelling isn't just for movies or novels—it's one of the most powerful tools you have as a content creator. Stories captivate, inspire, and connect. They make your audience feel something, and that emotional connection is what keeps them engaged.

1. Hook Your Audience Early

The first few seconds of your content are crucial. Whether it's a video, podcast, or blog post, you need to grab your audience's attention right away. This is your hook—the thing that makes them want to stick around and see what you have to say.

Start with something that piques curiosity, poses a question, or addresses a problem your audience is facing. For example, if you're creating a video on productivity, you might start with, "Do you feel like there are never enough hours in the day? Here's how to get more done in less time." The goal is to make your audience think, "I need to hear this."

2. Use Relatable Stories

Your stories don't have to be epic—they just have to be relatable. Share personal anecdotes, experiences, and challenges that your audience can see themselves in. Maybe it's the time you started a project and failed miserably, or the day you had an aha moment that changed everything.

Relatable stories make you human, and they remind your audience that you're not just a content creator—you're a real person who's been through ups and downs, just like them.

3. Build a Narrative Arc

Even short-form content can benefit from a narrative arc. A narrative arc is the structure of your story—how it starts, builds, and ends. Think of it as the journey you're taking your audience on. The basic structure includes:

1. **Introduction:** Set the stage and introduce the main idea or conflict.
2. **Rising Action:** Build tension or excitement as you delve deeper into the topic.
3. **Climax:** This is the peak of your story—the big reveal, the turning point, or the main takeaway.
4. **Falling Action:** Start to wrap things up, providing solutions or lessons learned.
5. **Conclusion:** End with a strong closing statement, call-to-action, or final thought that leaves your audience feeling inspired, informed, or entertained.

Even in a short TikTok video, this structure can be applied in just a few sentences or actions.

4. Make Your Audience the Hero

One of the best ways to engage your audience is by making them the hero of your story. Instead of positioning yourself as the all-knowing expert, position your audience as the one on a journey, and you're simply their guide.

For example, instead of saying, "I'm going to show you how to lose weight," try saying, "You're going to learn how to lose weight and feel amazing." It's a subtle shift, but it makes your audience feel like they're the star of the show, and you're just here to help them shine.

5. Use Visual and Sensory Language

When you're telling a story, the details matter. Use descriptive language that paints a picture in your audience's mind. Instead of saying, "It was a tough day," say, "I felt the weight of the world on my shoulders as I walked through the door, exhausted and over-whelmed." See the difference? The second version makes you feel something.

You can also use sensory language—talk about how things looked, sounded, smelled, tasted, or felt. The more senses you engage, the more immersive your storytelling will be.

6. End with Impact

The end of your story is just as important as the beginning. Don't just let your content fizzle out—end with impact. Whether it's a powerful call-to-action, a thought-provoking question, or a heartfelt statement, leave your audience with something that sticks. You want them to feel something, do something, or think differently because of your content.

Visual and Audio Content Tips: The Art of Getting Views

Now that we've covered storytelling, let's talk about the technical side—how to make your content visually and audibly engaging. In the creator economy, presentation matters. High-quality visuals and clear audio aren't just nice to have—they're essential for capturing and retaining your audience's attention.

1. Invest in Quality Gear (But Don't Break the Bank)

You don't need to spend thousands of dollars on equipment to create great content, but investing in some basic gear can make a big difference. Here's what to consider:

- **Camera:** Your smartphone camera is often good enough to start, especially with the latest models. If you want to upgrade, look for a DSLR or mirrorless camera that fits your budget and needs.
- **Microphone:** Audio quality is just as important—if not more important—than video quality. A good microphone can instantly make your content sound more professional. Consider a lapel mic, a USB mic for desktop recording, or a shotgun mic for on-camera work.
- **Lighting:** Good lighting can elevate your content instantly. Natural light is great, but if you're filming indoors, invest in some affordable softbox lights or ring lights to keep your shots well-lit and visually appealing.

2. Master Your Editing Software

Editing is where the magic happens. It's where you bring all the pieces together, cut out the fluff, and add the polish that makes your content shine. Take the time to learn your editing software, whether it's Adobe Premiere, Final Cut Pro, iMovie, or something else. Editing can be daunting at first, but the more you practice, the better you'll get.

Here are some quick tips:

- **Cut the Fat:** Attention spans are short. Trim out anything that doesn't add value or move the story forward.
- **Add B-Roll:** B-roll footage—those extra clips that complement your main content—can make your videos more dynamic and engaging. Use B-roll to illustrate what you're talking about or to keep the visuals interesting.
- **Use Music and Sound Effects:** Music sets the tone and adds energy to your content. Choose tracks that match the mood you're going for, and don't forget to adjust the volume so it doesn't overpower your voice. Sound effects can also add emphasis or humor.

3. Optimize for Mobile Viewing

A huge portion of your audience is likely watching on their phones, so make sure your content is optimized for mobile. This means using vertical or square formats for social media, keeping text large and readable, and ensuring your visuals are clear on smaller screens.

4. Play with Visuals: Text, Graphics, and Animations

Adding text, graphics, and animations can make your content more engaging and help convey your message. Use text overlays to highlight key points, create infographics to break down complex information, or add animations to keep the visuals lively.

But remember, less is often more. Don't overcrowd your content with too many effects—it should enhance, not distract.

5. Keep Your Audio Crisp and Clear

There's nothing more off-putting than bad audio. If your audience can't hear you clearly, they're going to click away fast. Record in a quiet space, use a good mic, and edit out any background noise or distractions. If you're recording outside, consider using a windscreen for your mic to minimize wind noise.

6. Use Thumbnails and Titles That Pop

Your thumbnail and title are the first things people see, and they play a huge role in whether someone clicks on your content. Thumbnails should be eye-catching, with clear, bold text and a compelling image that reflects the content. Your title should be intriguing and promise value—something that makes your audience think, "I need to watch this."

Leveraging AI and Smart Technology for Content Creation: Tools to Save Time and Enhance Quality

Technology is your friend, especially when it comes to content creation. AI and smart tools can help you streamline your workflow, improve your quality, and even come up with fresh ideas. Let's look at some ways you can use technology to your advantage.

1. AI-Powered Editing Tools

Editing can be time-consuming, but AI-powered tools are changing the game. Apps like Descript allow you to edit video and audio as easily as editing text, automatically removing filler words and generating captions. Tools like Adobe's Sensei use AI to help with color correction, sound balancing, and even video resizing for different platforms.

2. Content Planning and Idea Generation

If you're ever stuck for ideas, AI tools like ChatGPT can help you brainstorm content topics, generate outlines, or even write draft scripts. Tools like BuzzSumo analyze what's trending in your niche, while AnswerThePublic shows you the questions people are asking online. Use these insights to create content that's timely, relevant, and in demand.

3. Automate Your Workflow

Automation tools can save you tons of time by handling repetitive tasks. Tools like Zapier or IFTTT can connect your apps and automate actions like posting to social media, sending email reminders, or organizing files. Social media schedulers like Buffer or Later allow you to plan and schedule your posts in advance, so you're not scrambling to post every day.

4. Enhance Your Visuals with AI

AI-driven design tools like Canva Pro and Adobe Spark make it easy to create professional-looking graphics, thumbnails, and social media posts without a design background. You can also use tools like Lumen5 to turn your blog posts into engaging videos, or DALL-E to generate unique images for your content.

5. Transcriptions and Captions

Adding captions to your videos is essential for accessibility and keeping viewers engaged, especially those watching without sound. AI tools like Otter.ai or Rev make transcription quick and easy, allowing you to add captions or create text-based content from your audio and video files.

6. SEO Optimization Tools

SEO isn't just for websites—it's crucial for getting your content seen on platforms like YouTube and even Instagram. Tools like TubeBuddy and VidIQ can help you optimize your video titles, tags, and descriptions to improve your ranking. For blog posts, use Yoast or SEMrush to ensure your content is optimized for search engines.

7. Analytics and Performance Tracking

Knowing how your content is performing is key to improving and growing. Use analytics tools to track views, engagement, watch time, and other key metrics. Google Analytics, YouTube Analytics, and platform-specific insights will show you what's working and what's not, helping you refine your strategy over time.

Creating engaging content isn't just about what you post—it's about how you plan, execute, and refine your approach. By using storytelling, focusing on high-quality visuals and audio, and leveraging technology, you can create content that not only grabs attention but also builds lasting connections with your audience. Remember, every piece of content is an opportunity to tell your story, share your expertise, and make an impact.

Now, go out there and create something amazing.

CHAPTER 5

GROWING YOUR AUDIENCE

Alright, creators, let's get into one of the most crucial aspects of your journey in the creator economy—growing your audience. You've got the content, the brand, and the passion, but if no one's watching, listening, or reading, then it's like performing on stage to an empty theater. Growing your audience isn't just about vanity metrics like likes and follows—it's about building a community that's genuinely connected to you and your message. It's about creating a loyal fanbase that supports you, buys your products, shares your content, and sticks with you for the long haul.

In this chapter, we're going to dive into the nuts and bolts of how to grow your audience. From optimizing your social media profiles and using SEO tactics to engaging with your followers and analyzing your data, we're going to cover everything you need to know to take your audience growth to the next level. So let's get into it!

Social Media Optimization (SEO for Social Media): Boosting Your Reach

When we talk about SEO (Search Engine Optimization), most people think of Google and websites, but SEO isn't just for bloggers and businesses. It's a game-changer for social media too. Think of social media SEO as the secret sauce that helps your content get discovered. It's about making sure your posts, profiles, and videos are optimized so they show up when people search for topics related to your niche.

1. Optimize Your Profile

Let's start with the basics—your social media profile. Whether it's Instagram, TikTok, YouTube, or any other platform, your profile is the first impression people get of you, so make it count.

- **Username:** Keep it simple, memorable, and consistent across all platforms. If your brand name is taken, try adding "official" or "real" to your username, but avoid numbers and unnecessary characters that make it hard to find you.
- **Bio:** Your bio is your elevator pitch. Use it to clearly explain who you are, what you do, and why people should follow you. Include keywords related to your niche and a call-to-action, like a link to your website, latest video, or an email sign-up.

- **Profile Picture:** Choose a profile picture that's clear, recognizable, and reflects your brand. It could be a professional photo of you, your logo, or something that visually represents what you're about. Keep it consistent across platforms so people immediately recognize you.
- **Links:** Use the link in your bio wisely. On platforms like Instagram, where you only get one clickable link, use a tool like Linktree or Beacons to create a mini landing page with multiple links to your content, shop, or services.

2. Use Keywords Wisely

Keywords aren't just for blog posts—they're crucial on social media too. Think about the words your audience might type in when searching for content like yours, and incorporate those keywords into your profile, posts, and captions.

- **Hashtags:** Hashtags are keywords for social media, and they help categorize your content and make it discoverable. Use a mix of popular, niche, and branded hashtags in your posts. But don't go overboard—too many hashtags can look spammy. Aim for 5-10 relevant hashtags per post.
- **Captions and Descriptions:** Use captions and video descriptions to add context and include keywords naturally. For YouTube videos, fill out the description box thoroughly with relevant keywords, timestamps, and links. For Instagram and TikTok, include keywords early in your

caption since only the first few lines are visible without clicking "more."

3. Utilize Alt Text and Closed Captions

Alt text isn't just for accessibility—it's also an SEO tool. On Instagram, you can add alt text to your images, which tells the platform what the image is about, helping your posts rank in search results. Similarly, adding closed captions to videos not only makes them more accessible but also helps with SEO because platforms like YouTube use that text to understand your content better.

4. Geotags and Location-Based SEO

If you're a local business, influencer, or creator looking to connect with your community, use geotags to boost your local SEO. Tag your location in your posts and stories so people in your area can discover your content. This is especially useful for creators like food bloggers, travel vloggers, or anyone offering location-based content.

5. Leverage Trending Topics and Challenges

One of the best ways to boost your reach is by jumping on trending topics, challenges, or hashtags. Whether it's a viral dance challenge on TikTok, a trending meme on Instagram, or a popular topic on Twitter, participating in trends shows that you're active, relevant, and in tune with what's happening now.

Just make sure the trend aligns with your brand. You don't want to jump on every bandwagon just for the sake of it—pick trends that make sense for your niche and audience.

6. Create Shareable Content

Content that gets shared is content that grows. When your audience shares your posts, it exposes you to a whole new group of potential followers. To make your content shareable, think about what would make someone want to send it to a friend—funny memes, insightful tips, relatable quotes, or jaw-dropping visuals are all great for sharing.

Use calls-to-action in your captions to encourage sharing. Simple phrases like "Tag a friend who needs to see this" or "Share this with someone who loves [insert topic]" can boost your shares.

Techniques for Growing Followers: Organic vs. Paid Strategies

Now that you've optimized your profiles, let's talk about how to actually grow your follower count. There are two main strategies: organic and paid. Both have their pros and cons, and the best approach often combines elements of both.

Organic Growth Strategies

Organic growth means gaining followers naturally without spending money on ads. It's the dream scenario, but it also takes time, effort, and consistency. Here's how to grow your audience organically:

1. Post Consistently

Consistency is the name of the game. Social media algorithms love consistency because it signals that you're an active user, which means your content is more likely to be shown to others. Whether it's once a day, three times a week, or whatever schedule works for you, stick to it.

Consistency isn't just about frequency; it's also about style and tone. Your audience should know what to expect when they come to your page. If you're known for motivational quotes, keep them coming. If it's educational content, keep providing value. Consistency builds trust, and trust keeps people coming back.

2. Collaborate with Other Creators

Collaboration is one of the most effective ways to grow your audience organically. When you team up with another creator, you're essentially sharing each other's audiences. Whether it's a joint Instagram Live, a YouTube collab, or a guest appearance on someone's podcast, collaborations expose you to new potential followers who already trust the person you're collaborating with.

Choose collaborators whose audience aligns with yours. It doesn't have to be someone with millions of followers—even small creators can have highly engaged audiences that are eager to discover new voices.

3. Engage with Your Community

Engagement goes both ways. If you want people to engage with your content, you need to engage with theirs. Respond to comments, like and share your followers' posts, and join in on conversations within your niche. The more active you are, the more visible you'll be.

Don't just engage on your own posts—engage with other creators in your space. Comment on their posts, participate in their discussions, and become a familiar face in your niche community. This helps you build connections and gets your name in front of a wider audience.

4. Use Giveaways and Contests

Giveaways and contests are a great way to boost engagement and attract new followers. People love the chance to win something, and they're often willing to follow, like, and share your content to enter.

Make sure your giveaway prize is something that appeals to your target audience. It could be a product, a service, or even something digital like a free e-book or a 1-on-1 consultation. Use your giveaway as an opportunity to grow your email list, encourage shares, or boost your engagement.

5. Create Evergreen Content

Evergreen content is content that stays relevant over time—think how-to guides, tips, and educational posts that people can return to again and again. Evergreen content continues to attract traffic long after it's posted, making it a valuable tool for growing your audience organically.

For example, a YouTube video on "how to start a podcast" will always be relevant as long as people are interested in podcasting. Contrast that with a trending challenge that might be popular for a week and then forgotten. A mix of evergreen and trending content keeps your audience engaged while attracting new followers over time.

6. Optimize Your Content for Shareability

We talked about creating shareable content, but let's dig a little deeper. Shareability isn't just about what you post—it's about how you package it. Use bold visuals, compelling headlines, and clear calls-to-action that make people want to share.

Infographics, carousels, and bite-sized videos often perform well because they're easy to consume and share. Think about how you can present your content in a way that makes people excited to pass it along.

Paid Growth Strategies

Paid growth involves using advertising dollars to promote your content, reach new audiences, and grow your followers. The great thing about paid growth is that it's fast—you can see results almost immediately. The downside? It costs money, and if you're not strategic, it can get expensive quickly.

1. Paid Social Media Ads

Most social media platforms offer paid ad options that let you promote your content to specific audiences. You can run ads on Instagram, Facebook, TikTok, YouTube, and more. The key is targeting—make sure your ads are reaching the right people.

Experiment with different ad formats, like video ads, carousel ads, or story ads, to see what resonates with your audience. Start with a small budget to test different creatives and audiences before scaling up your spending.

2. Influencer Partnerships

Another paid strategy is to work with influencers who can promote your content to their audience. This doesn't always mean paying for a shoutout—sometimes it's about offering something of value in return, like free products, services, or a commission on sales.

Choose influencers who have an audience that aligns with your brand, and make sure their engagement is genuine. An influencer with a smaller but highly engaged audience can be more valuable than one with millions of followers who rarely interact.

3. Sponsored Posts and Boosting Content

Sponsored posts are another way to get your content seen by more people. Platforms like Facebook and Instagram allow you to boost posts, which means paying to show your existing content to a broader audience.

This is a great option if you have a piece of content that's already performing well organically and you want to give it an extra push. It's also a good way to promote new content to people who don't follow you yet.

Engaging with Your Audience: Building a Community, Not Just a Following

Growing your audience isn't just about getting more followers— it's about building a community. Your audience should feel like they're part of something bigger, not just passive consumers of your content. When you create a sense of community, your followers become more loyal, more engaged, and more likely to support you in the long run.

1. Be Present and Responsive

One of the easiest ways to build a community is by being present and responsive. Don't just post and disappear—stick around to interact with your audience. Respond to comments, answer questions, and acknowledge your followers when they engage with your content.

People love to feel seen and heard, and when you take the time to respond, it shows that you value your community. Even a simple "thanks for your comment!" can go a long way in making your followers feel appreciated.

2. Host Live Sessions and Q&As

Live sessions are one of the best ways to connect with your audience in real-time. Whether it's a live Q&A, a product demo, or just a casual chat, going live allows you to interact with your audience directly, answer their questions, and build deeper connections.

Platforms like Instagram, TikTok, YouTube, and Facebook all offer live streaming options, and it's a great way to humanize your brand and show your personality. Plus, live sessions create a sense of urgency—people don't want to miss out, so they're more likely to tune in.

3. Create a Safe Space for Conversations

Your social media pages aren't just about you—they're about your community. Encourage your followers to share their thoughts, ask questions, and start discussions. Create a safe space where people feel comfortable engaging, and moderate your comments to keep the conversation respectful and positive.

Consider starting a private Facebook group, Discord server, or Slack channel where your most loyal followers can connect with each other and with you. This gives them a space to dive deeper into your content, share their own experiences, and feel like part of a supportive community.

4. Share User-Generated Content

One of the best ways to show your audience that you appreciate them is by sharing their content. If someone tags you in a post, shares a testimonial, or uses your product, highlight them on your page. This not only boosts their visibility but also shows your community that you value their support.

User-generated content adds credibility to your brand and encourages more followers to engage. It's a win-win—your audience gets recognized, and you get authentic content to share.

5. Ask for Feedback and Listen

Your audience isn't just there to consume your content—they're there to be a part of it. Ask for their feedback, whether it's through polls, questions, or direct messages. What do they like? What do they want to see more of? What could you be doing better?

Listening to your audience's feedback shows that you care about their experience and are willing to adapt. Plus, it gives you valuable insights that can help you refine your content and strategy.

6. Be Authentic and Relatable

Authenticity is the key to building a loyal community. Be yourself, share your journey, and don't be afraid to show the ups and downs. When you're authentic, your audience feels like they know you, and that connection is what turns casual followers into dedicated fans.

Remember, your community isn't just numbers on a screen— they're real people. Treat them with respect, engage with them genuinely, and build relationships that go beyond likes and comments.

Analyzing Data and Insights for Continuous Improvement

Growing your audience is an ongoing process, and one of the best ways to keep improving is by analyzing your data. Your analytics tell the story of what's working, what's not, and where you can make adjustments to better serve your audience.

1. Track Your Key Metrics

Not all metrics are created equal. While likes and follows are great, they're not the only indicators of success. Pay attention to key metrics like engagement rate, reach, impressions, and click-through rates. These metrics give you a clearer picture of how your audience is interacting with your content.

- **Engagement Rate:** This shows how actively your audience is engaging with your content. High engagement means people are liking, commenting, sharing, and saving your posts—a good sign that your content is resonating.
- **Reach and Impressions:** Reach tells you how many unique users have seen your content, while impressions show how many times it's been viewed. High reach with low engagement might mean your content is getting seen but not compelling enough to interact with.
- **Click-Through Rate (CTR):** If you're using links in your content, your CTR tells you how many people are clicking through to your website, shop, or other destinations. A high CTR indicates that your content is driving action.

2. Use Platform-Specific Analytics Tools

Every social media platform comes with its own analytics tools, and they're gold mines of information. Dive into YouTube Analytics, Instagram Insights, Facebook Page Insights, or TikTok Analytics to get detailed data on your content's performance.

Look for patterns—what types of posts get the most likes? When is your audience most active? What topics do they engage with the most? Use this data to refine your content strategy and focus on what works.

3. Experiment and Adapt

Social media is always evolving, and so is your audience. What worked last month might not work today, and that's okay. The key is to keep experimenting, testing new ideas, and adapting to changes in the platform algorithms and audience behavior.

Try new content formats, post at different times, or switch up your style to see how your audience responds. Treat every piece of content as an experiment, and don't be afraid to pivot when needed.

4. Set Goals and Measure Progress

Growth doesn't happen overnight, and it's easy to get discouraged if you don't see immediate results. Set realistic goals for your audience growth and measure your progress regularly. Celebrate the small wins—whether it's hitting your first 1,000 followers, reaching a new engagement milestone, or getting your first brand partnership.

Use your goals as motivation to keep pushing forward, and remember that audience growth is a marathon, not a sprint.

5. Learn from Your Mistakes

Not every piece of content will be a hit, and that's okay. The key is to learn from your mistakes. If a post doesn't perform well, don't just shrug it off—analyze why. Was it the timing? The visuals? The messaging? Use every misstep as an opportunity to learn and improve.

Failure is part of the process, and every creator experiences it at some point. What sets successful creators apart is their willingness to learn, adapt, and keep going.

6. Keep Evolving

The creator economy is constantly changing, and the best creators evolve with it. Stay up-to-date on new trends, platform updates, and audience behavior. Keep learning, keep experimenting, and never get too comfortable. The more you evolve, the more you'll grow, and the stronger your audience will become.

Growing your audience isn't just about numbers—it's about creating a community that's connected, engaged, and invested in what you do. By optimizing your social media presence, using smart growth strategies, engaging deeply with your audience, and analyzing your data, you can build a loyal following that supports your brand and helps you thrive in the creator economy. So keep showing up, keep sharing, and keep growing.

Your audience is out there—now it's time to find them.

CHAPTER 6

MONETIZING YOUR INFLUENCE

Alright, creators, it's time to talk about money. You've put in the work to build your brand, grow your audience, and create content that resonates. Now, it's time to turn that influence into income. Monetizing your influence is what takes you from a passionate creator to a full-blown business owner. It's where your creativity meets entrepreneurship, and the opportunities are endless if you know where to look.

Whether you're just starting to think about making money from your content or you're looking to diversify your income streams, this chapter will guide you through the different ways to monetize your influence. We'll cover everything from sponsored content and affiliate marketing to product sales, brand partnerships, and beyond. Plus, we'll dive into the nitty-gritty of negotiating deals, staying compliant with legal guidelines, and presenting yourself professionally with a killer media kit. Let's get into it!

Revenue Streams for Creators: Sponsored Content, Affiliate Marketing, Product Sales, and More

The beauty of the creator economy is that there are countless ways to make money. You're not limited to just one income stream—you can stack multiple revenue sources to create a sustainable and scalable business. Let's break down some of the most popular ways creators are monetizing their influence.

1. Sponsored Content

Sponsored content is one of the most common revenue streams for creators, and it's also one of the most lucrative. Brands pay you to create content that promotes their products or services, and it's a win-win because you get paid to share something you (hopefully) genuinely love with your audience.

Sponsored content can take many forms: Instagram posts, YouTube videos, TikTok clips, blog articles, or even podcast mentions. The key to successful sponsored content is authenticity—your audience can tell when you're genuinely excited about a product versus when you're just doing it for the paycheck. Always choose partnerships that align with your brand and provide value to your followers.

How to Get Started with Sponsored Content:

- **Build Your Portfolio:** Before you can land paid sponsorships, you need to showcase your work. Create content that features products you love, even if you're not getting paid yet. These pieces will serve as examples of what you can offer brands.

- **Reach Out to Brands:** Don't be afraid to pitch yourself to brands directly. Create a list of companies that align with your niche and reach out via email or social media with a pitch that includes who you are, what you do, your audience demographics, and why you're a good fit.

- **Join Influencer Platforms:** Platforms like AspireIQ, CreatorIQ, and Influencer.co connect creators with brands looking for sponsorships. Sign up, create a profile, and start applying for opportunities.

2. Affiliate Marketing

Affiliate marketing is another popular way to make money, and it's perfect for creators who want to recommend products they genuinely love. Here's how it works: you promote a product or service using a unique affiliate link, and when someone makes a purchase through that link, you earn a commission. It's a great way to monetize your influence without creating your own products.

How to Get Started with Affiliate Marketing:

- **Join Affiliate Programs:** Many companies have affiliate programs, from Amazon Associates to niche-specific brands. Sign up for programs that align with your content and audience.

- **Use Your Links Strategically:** Place your affiliate links in your YouTube video descriptions, blog posts, social media bios, or even swipe-up links on Instagram Stories. Just be sure to disclose that the links are affiliate links (more on that later).
- **Promote Authentically:** Your audience can tell when you're just pushing products to make a commission. Only promote items you genuinely love and believe in, and always be transparent about your affiliations.

3. Product Sales: Digital and Physical

Creating and selling your own products is one of the best ways to take full control of your income. The possibilities are endless—digital products like e-books, courses, and printables are low-cost to create and can generate passive income. Physical products like merchandise, art prints, or handcrafted items allow you to share a piece of your brand in a tangible way.

How to Get Started with Product Sales:

- **Identify Your Audience's Needs:** Think about what your audience would find valuable. Are they looking for more in-depth knowledge? Create an online course. Are they asking where you got your hoodie? Launch a merch line.
- **Use E-commerce Platforms:** Sites like Shopify, Etsy, Gumroad, and Teachable make it easy to set up an online

store or host digital products. They handle payments, downloads, and logistics, so you can focus on creating.

- **Promote Your Products:** Use your existing content channels to promote your products. Create dedicated posts, share behind-the-scenes of the creation process, and offer exclusive discounts to your followers.

4. Memberships and Subscriptions

Memberships and subscriptions are all about creating exclusive content for your most loyal fans. Platforms like Patreon, Ko-fi, and Substack allow you to offer perks like early access, exclusive videos, or members-only Q&As in exchange for a monthly fee. This recurring revenue model provides stability and fosters a closer relationship with your audience.

How to Get Started with Memberships:

- **Decide What You'll Offer:** Your membership perks should provide value that goes beyond your free content. Think exclusive tutorials, personalized advice, bonus episodes, or private community access.
- **Set Your Pricing:** Start with a tiered pricing model, offering different levels of access at different price points. This allows you to cater to a wider range of followers.
- **Promote and Engage:** Regularly promote your membership options on your social media and keep your members engaged with consistent updates and exclusive perks. Make them feel like they're part of an inner circle.

5. Ad Revenue

If you're a YouTuber or podcaster, ad revenue can be a significant income stream. Platforms like YouTube pay creators based on ad views through their Partner Program, while podcasters can earn through programmatic ads or direct sponsorships. It's a more passive form of income that grows as your audience does.

How to Get Started with Ad Revenue:

- **Meet Platform Requirements:** For YouTube, you need at least 1,000 subscribers and 4,000 watch hours in the past year to join the Partner Program. Other platforms have similar requirements, so make sure you're eligible.
- **Create Content that's Ad-Friendly:** Be mindful of platform guidelines regarding monetization. Avoid content that's too controversial, explicit, or in violation of community standards, as this can impact your ad revenue.
- **Explore Additional Ad Networks:** Besides platform ads, you can join networks like AdSense, Media.net, or other ad exchanges that pay for traffic to your site or channel.

6. Public Speaking and Workshops

As your influence grows, opportunities to speak at events, host workshops, or offer coaching may arise. These gigs can be highly lucrative and also help position you as an expert in your field.

How to Get Started with Public Speaking:

- **Build Your Speaking Resume:** Start small by offering free webinars, joining podcast panels, or speaking at local meetups. As you gain experience, you can start pitching yourself for paid gigs.
- **Create a Speaker's Kit:** Similar to a media kit, a speaker's kit highlights your experience, topics you cover, and testimonials from past events. This will make you look professional and prepared when reaching out to event organizers.

Negotiating Brand Partnerships and Sponsorship Deals: Knowing Your Worth

Now that you know about the different ways to make money, let's talk about how to get those deals locked in—especially when it comes to brand partnerships and sponsorships. Negotiating can be intimidating, especially if you're new to the game, but knowing your worth is crucial. Brands are looking to leverage your audience and influence, so it's up to you to make sure you're getting fairly compensated for the value you provide.

1. Know Your Rates

The first step in negotiating is knowing what to charge. Rates can vary widely depending on factors like your audience size, engagement rate, niche, and the scope of work. A common formula to start with is to charge $100 per 10,000 followers on Instagram for a single post, but this is just a rough guideline. Your rates should reflect the value you bring, not just the numbers.

Factors to Consider When Setting Your Rates:

- **Engagement Rate:** A highly engaged audience is often more valuable than a larger, less active one. Brands want to see that your followers interact with your content, not just scroll past it.
- **Content Format:** Videos usually command higher rates than static posts because they take more time and effort to create. If you're producing reels, long-form videos, or podcasts, make sure you're charging accordingly.
- **Exclusivity and Usage Rights:** If a brand wants exclusivity (meaning you can't work with their competitors), or if they want to use your content for ads, you should charge more. Usage rights can add significant value to your content, so don't give them away for free.
- **Deliverables and Time Commitment:** The more deliverables required—such as multiple posts, stories, or cross-platform promotion—the higher your rate should be. Also, factor in the time commitment for filming, editing, and revisions.

2. Be Transparent About Your Value

When negotiating, be clear about the value you bring to the table. Highlight your engagement rates, audience demographics, past successful collaborations, and the unique touch you add to your content. Brands want to know what they're paying for, so don't be shy about showcasing your results.

Provide case studies or examples of how previous partnerships have benefited both you and the brands you've worked with. This builds credibility and justifies your rates.

3. Don't Undersell Yourself

One of the biggest mistakes creators make is accepting low rates out of fear of losing the deal. While it's tempting to say yes to anything when you're just starting out, consistently accepting lower pay sets a precedent that's hard to break. Know your worth and be prepared to walk away if a brand isn't willing to meet your rates.

It's better to have fewer well-paid partnerships than to be overworked for peanuts. Remember, your influence has value, and brands know that. Stand firm in your negotiations, and don't compromise on your rates just to close a deal.

4. Negotiate Beyond Cash: Value Additions

Money isn't the only thing on the table. When negotiating, consider value additions like affiliate commissions, performance bonuses, cross-promotion on the brand's platforms, or additional perks like free products, event tickets, or travel accommodations.

For example, if a brand can't meet your cash rate, suggest alternative compensation like a higher commission rate on affiliate sales or bonus payments for hitting certain performance metrics. These extras can often make up for a lower upfront payment.

5. Get Everything in Writing

Always, always, always get your agreements in writing. A contract protects both you and the brand, outlining the deliverables, payment terms, usage rights, deadlines, and any exclusivity agreements. Don't rely on verbal agreements or casual emails—formalize everything in a contract to avoid misunderstandings.

If a brand doesn't provide a contract, draft one yourself or use a simple influencer agreement template that covers the basics. It's better to be safe than sorry, especially when money and legal rights are involved.

Legal Aspects and Disclosure Guidelines: Keeping It Above Board

Monetizing your influence comes with legal responsibilities, especially when it comes to sponsored content and affiliate marketing. Staying compliant isn't just about following the rules—it's about building trust with your audience. Let's go over the key legal aspects and disclosure guidelines every creator should know.

1. Disclosure Guidelines: Be Transparent

Transparency is the name of the game when it comes to sponsored content and affiliate links. Your audience deserves to know when you're getting paid to promote a product, and failing to disclose can land you in hot water with regulatory bodies like the Federal Trade Commission (FTC) in the U.S.

How to Properly Disclose:

- **Use Clear Language:** Phrases like "#ad," "#sponsored," or "paid partnership" are simple and effective. Avoid vague terms like "thanks to [brand]" which don't clearly indicate a paid relationship.
- **Place Disclosures Prominently:** Disclosures should be visible and easy to understand. On Instagram, this means placing it in the first line of your caption, not buried at the bottom. On YouTube, mention it verbally in the video and include it in the description.
- **Disclose Affiliate Links:** If you're using affiliate links, make sure to disclose that you'll earn a commission if someone makes a purchase. Phrases like "I may earn a small commission at no extra cost to you" are straightforward and transparent.

2. Protecting Your Intellectual Property

Your content is your intellectual property, and you have the right to control how it's used. Be mindful of brands asking for full usage rights or the ability to repurpose your content across their channels without additional compensation. These rights are valuable, and you should charge accordingly if brands want to use your content beyond your platform.

Clearly outline usage rights in your contracts. Specify how long the brand can use your content, on which platforms, and whether they can modify it. If the brand wants to run ads with your content, that's an additional usage right that should come with a higher fee.

3. Managing Taxes and Business Structure

As a creator, you're essentially running your own business, which means you need to handle taxes, business expenses, and income tracking. Depending on where you live, you may need to set aside a portion of your earnings for taxes and consider forming a business entity like an LLC for liability protection.

Tips for Managing Taxes:

- **Track Your Income and Expenses:** Use tools like QuickBooks, FreshBooks, or even a simple spreadsheet to track every dollar earned and spent. This will make tax season a lot less stressful.
- **Set Aside Money for Taxes:** A good rule of thumb is to set aside 20-30% of your income for taxes. This ensures you're not caught off guard when it's time to pay.
- **Hire a Professional:** If managing taxes and business finances feels overwhelming, consider hiring an accountant who understands the creator economy. They can help you with tax planning, deductions, and compliance.

Creating Effective Media Kits: Presenting Yourself Professionally to Brands

Your media kit is like your resume for brand partnerships—it showcases who you are, what you do, and why brands should work with you. A well-designed media kit not only highlights your stats and achievements but also tells your story and sets you apart from other creators. Let's go over how to create a media kit that impresses.

1. What to Include in Your Media Kit

A media kit should be comprehensive yet concise. Here's what you should include:

- **About You:** Start with a brief bio that tells your story, your niche, and what sets you apart. This is your chance to connect with brands on a personal level, so let your personality shine.
- **Audience Demographics:** Include key stats about your audience, such as age, gender, location, and interests. Brands want to know if your followers align with their target market.
- **Social Media Stats:** Highlight your follower count, engagement rate, average views, and any other relevant metrics. Use screenshots from platform analytics for credibility.
- **Content Examples:** Showcase some of your best work—this could be links to past sponsored posts,

standout content pieces, or case studies that demonstrate your impact.

- **Services and Pricing:** Outline the types of collaborations you offer (e.g., Instagram posts, TikTok videos, blog features) and include a general price range. You don't need to list exact rates—just give brands an idea of what to expect.

- **Testimonials and Past Collaborations:** If you've worked with brands before, include testimonials or logos from past clients. This builds credibility and shows that you have experience.

- **Contact Information:** Make it easy for brands to reach you. Include your email, social media handles, and any other relevant contact info.

2. Design Tips for Your Media Kit

Your media kit should look professional and reflect your brand's aesthetic. Use a clean, easy-to-read layout with consistent fonts, colors, and imagery that align with your overall brand.

- **Use High-Quality Visuals:** Include high-resolution images that represent your brand and your best content. Avoid clutter—keep the design sleek and focused.

- **Keep It Concise:** A media kit should be no more than 3-5 pages. You want to provide enough information to showcase your value without overwhelming brands with too much text.

- **Update Regularly:** Your media kit isn't a one-and-done project. Update it regularly with your latest stats, recent collaborations, and fresh content examples. Brands want to see your most current achievements.

3. How to Share Your Media Kit

When reaching out to brands, attach your media kit to your initial email pitch or provide a link to a downloadable version. You can also have it available on your website or a dedicated page on your Linktree for easy access.

Your media kit is a reflection of your professionalism and your value as a creator. It's the first impression brands get of you, so make it count.

Monetizing your influence is all about knowing your worth, exploring different revenue streams, and presenting yourself professionally to brands. Whether you're negotiating your first sponsorship deal, launching your own product line, or diving into affiliate marketing, the opportunities are there—you just have to seize them.

Remember, you're not just a creator—you're a business owner. Approach every partnership with confidence, protect your rights, and always keep your audience's trust at the forefront. Your influence is valuable, and with the right strategy, you can turn it into a thriving business.

Now go out there and get paid for the value you bring to the table.

CHAPTER 7

BUILDING A PROFESSIONAL BRAND: THE HIDDEN KEYS TO SUCCESS IN THE CREATOR ECONOMY

S o, you've nailed the art of content creation, mastered the game of growing your audience, and even figured out how to start making money from your influence. But let's get real for a second: all of that hard work can be undone if you're not handling your business like a professional. This chapter is all about the stuff that doesn't get talked about enough—the behind-the-scenes moves that separate the hobbyists from the real players.

Being a successful creator is about more than just going viral or landing that big brand deal. It's about how you conduct yourself, how you manage your business, and how you build a team to take you to the next level. We're going to break down the importance of surrounding yourself with the right people, treating yourself like a business, and why professionalism isn't just a buzzword—it's a necessity. Plus, we'll dig into the economics of the creator world, and why understanding the business side of this industry is what's going to set you apart.

Building Your Dream Team: Why You Can't Do It All Yourself

When you're first starting out, it's natural to wear all the hats—you're the creator, editor, marketer, and manager all rolled into one. But at some point, if you're serious about scaling, you're going to need a team. You're going to need people who specialize in the areas where you don't, so you can focus on what you do best: creating.

1. The Power of Delegation: Letting Go of Control

Delegation isn't just about offloading tasks—it's about freeing up your time and mental energy to focus on the bigger picture. It's about putting your creative energy where it counts and trusting your team to handle the rest. As creators, we can be control freaks (hey, I've been there), but letting go is one of the smartest moves you'll ever make.

Why You Need to Delegate:

- **Focus on Creativity:** When you're caught up in editing, responding to emails, or negotiating deals, it's hard to stay in the creative flow. Delegating allows you to stay in your zone of genius and focus on creating high-quality content.

- **Boost Your Efficiency:** Your time is your most valuable asset. Delegating tasks to skilled professionals not only saves you time but also boosts the overall efficiency and quality of your work.

- **Scale Your Business:** There's a cap to how much you can do on your own. Delegation is essential for scaling your business and taking it to the next level. The sooner you realize you can't do it all, the faster you'll grow.

2. Key Team Members Every Creator Needs

As you grow, certain roles become crucial to your success. Let's talk about the key players you need on your team, why they matter, and how they'll help you scale your brand.

a. Manager: Your manager is your right hand, the person who handles the business side of things so you can stay focused on creating. A great manager will help you land brand deals, negotiate contracts, and keep your schedule running smoothly.

1. **What They Do:** Negotiate contracts, secure brand deals, handle business communications, and manage your calendar.

2. **When to Hire:** If you're feeling overwhelmed by business tasks, struggling to keep up with opportunities, or need help maximizing your revenue, it's time to bring on a manager.

b. Agent: An agent is similar to a manager but often focuses more on finding opportunities for you rather than handling the day-to-day management of your business. They can help land speaking engagements, book deals, and larger brand partnerships.

- **What They Do:** Scout opportunities, negotiate larger deals, and connect you with brands and companies that align with your brand.
- **When to Hire:** When you're ready to take your brand to bigger stages, like public speaking, publishing, or high-profile collaborations.

c. Videographer/Editor: Editing your own content can be a time drain, especially as your brand grows. Hiring a videographer or editor allows you to maintain high-quality content while freeing up your time to focus on other aspects of your business.

- **What They Do:** Film and edit your content, ensure a polished and professional look, and help bring your creative vision to life.
- **When to Hire:** When the time spent on editing is taking away from content creation or when you're ready to level up your production quality.

d. Social Media Manager: A social media manager handles the daily grind of posting, engaging, and growing your audience across platforms. They keep your social presence consistent, engaging, and aligned with your brand's voice.

- **What They Do:** Plan and schedule posts, engage with your audience, track social media analytics, and develop strategies to grow your platforms.
- **When to Hire:** When you're struggling to keep up with your posting schedule or want to implement a more strategic approach to your social media presence.

e. Virtual Assistant: A virtual assistant can take on a range of administrative tasks, from managing your inbox to coordinating with brands. They're a cost-effective way to handle the smaller tasks that still need to get done but don't necessarily require your personal touch.

- **What They Do:** Manage emails, schedule meetings, handle basic customer service, and assist with day-to-day operations.
- **When to Hire:** When you're losing hours each week to admin work that could be handled by someone else.

3. Finding the Right People: How to Build Your Team

Building your dream team isn't just about hiring anyone with a good resume—it's about finding people who understand your brand, your vision, and are committed to helping you grow. Here's how to go about it:

a. Know What You Need: Before you start looking for team members, be clear about what roles you need to fill and what specific skills you're looking for. Write down the tasks that are draining your time or require expertise that you don't have. This will help you identify the right people.

b. Hire for Fit, Not Just Skills: Your team is an extension of your brand, so hire people who share your values, understand your vision, and mesh well with your working style. Skills can be taught, but attitude and cultural fit are just as important.

c. Use Your Network: Reach out to other creators, attend industry events, and tap into your professional network to find the right talent. Personal recommendations often lead to the best hires.

d. Start Small: If you're hesitant to commit to full-time hires, start with freelancers or part-time contractors. This allows you to test the waters and ensure it's a good fit before making a bigger commitment.

What They Won't Tell You: The Unspoken Rules of Professionalism

Let's keep it real: you can have all the talent, strategy, and resources in the world, but if you're not handling your business professionally, it's all for nothing. Being a professional isn't just about showing up—it's about how you show up. It's about punctuality, reliability, and treating your brand like a business, not a side hustle. Here's the stuff they won't tell you, but you need to know.

1. Be Punctual: Time is Your Most Valuable Asset

Being on time isn't just about courtesy—it's about showing respect for others and for your own business. Punctuality is one of the most underrated aspects of professionalism, but it speaks volumes about your work ethic and your respect for other people's time.

The Impact of Being Late:

- **Damages Your Reputation:** When you're late, you send a message that your time is more important than everyone else's. Over time, this erodes trust and damages relationships with brands, collaborators, and your audience.
- **Missed Opportunities:** Being late for meetings, calls, or deadlines can cost you opportunities. Brands want to work with creators who are reliable and respectful of their time.

Action Step: Make punctuality a non-negotiable. Set reminders, plan ahead, and build buffers into your schedule to account for unexpected delays. Being on time is a simple yet powerful way to stand out in a crowded market.

2. Treat Yourself Like a Business

If you want to be treated like a business, you have to act like one. That means having systems, processes, and standards in place that ensure you operate at a professional level. It's about how you present yourself, how you communicate, and how you handle your finances.

Professionalism 101:

- **Email Etiquette:** Your emails are often the first impression brands or collaborators have of you. Keep them professional, clear, and timely. Proofread for typos, respond promptly, and use a professional email signature.
- **Contracts Are Non-Negotiable:** Never engage in a business deal without a contract. It protects both you and the brand, outlining deliverables, timelines, and payment terms. A contract is your safety net, and it's crucial for maintaining professionalism.
- **Respect Your Deadlines:** Meeting deadlines is not optional—it's mandatory. If you've committed to a brand, deliver on time, every time. Late submissions damage your credibility and can cost you future opportunities.

3. The Follow-Up Game: Keep It Tight

Don't just finish a project and move on. Follow up with the brands and collaborators you work with. A thank-you email, a quick check-in, or a request for feedback goes a long way. It shows that you care about the relationship, not just the transaction.

The Power of Following Up:

- **Builds Strong Relationships:** Following up shows that you value the relationship beyond just the deliverable. It's a chance to solidify your professional reputation and set the stage for future work.
- **Keeps You Top of Mind:** Brands work with creators they remember. A thoughtful follow-up keeps you on their radar for future opportunities.

Action Step: Create a follow-up system. Set reminders to check in after a project wraps up, and don't be afraid to ask if there's any additional feedback or upcoming opportunities.

Understanding the Economics of the Creator Economy

The reason why there's a "creator economy" in the first place is because of the economics behind it. Brands, platforms, and businesses see creators as the new marketing powerhouses, and there's big money being invested in this space. But it's not enough to just be a creator—you need to understand the business side of it all.

1. Why Brands Invest in Creators: The Business Behind the Content

Brands see creators as authentic voices that can reach audiences in a way traditional advertising can't. They invest in creators because of the trust, engagement, and influence that creators hold with their followers. But here's the kicker: brands aren't just buying your audience—they're buying your ability to drive economic value.

What Brands Look For:

- **Engagement Over Followers:** It's not just about having a million followers; it's about how engaged they are. Brands want to see that your audience listens, interacts, and responds to your content.
- **Professionalism and Reliability:** Brands want to work with creators who handle themselves like professionals. That means meeting deadlines, communicating clearly, and delivering high-quality work.
- **ROI (Return on Investment):** At the end of the day, brands are looking at the bottom line. Can you drive sales, generate leads, or create buzz? Understanding how your work contributes to their business goals will set you apart.

2. Thinking Like a Business: Focusing on the Economy, Not Just the Content

As a creator, it's easy to get caught up in the creative side and forget that you're also running a business. But to truly succeed, you need to think like a business owner. That means understanding the economics of what you're doing, from pricing your services correctly to knowing how to negotiate contracts that reflect your worth.

Key Business Principles for Creators:

- **Know Your Numbers:** Understand your revenue streams, expenses, and profit margins. Tracking your finances isn't just for tax season—it's crucial for making informed business decisions.

- **Set Clear Rates:** Don't guess when it comes to pricing your work. Know your rates, be clear about your terms, and don't be afraid to charge what you're worth. Confidence in your pricing is key to being taken seriously.

- **Scale Smartly:** Growth is exciting, but scaling too quickly can be risky. Make sure your business decisions are data-driven and sustainable. Invest in what will truly move the needle, and don't be afraid to say no to opportunities that don't align with your goals.

3. Leveraging Data and Analytics to Grow Your Brand

Data isn't just for tech companies—it's for you, too. Understanding your analytics gives you insights into what's working, what's not, and where you should focus your efforts. It's not about vanity metrics; it's about actionable data that helps you make smarter business decisions.

Using Data to Your Advantage:

- **Audience Insights:** Who is watching your content? What do they respond to? Use these insights to tailor your content, pitches, and brand partnerships to align with what your audience loves.
- **Performance Metrics:** Track the performance of your content across platforms. Look at engagement rates, watch time, click-through rates, and conversion rates. These metrics tell you what's resonating and where you can improve.
- **Test, Analyze, Repeat:** Don't be afraid to experiment with new formats, strategies, or platforms. Use data to test different approaches, analyze the results, and adjust accordingly. The creator economy rewards those who are willing to adapt and evolve.

Wrapping It All Up: Professionalism Is Your Superpower

Building a successful career in the creator economy is about so much more than just being talented or creating great content. It's about how you conduct yourself, how you treat your brand, and how seriously you take your business. The creators who win aren't just the most creative—they're the most professional, the most strategic, and the most dedicated to their craft.

So, build your team, treat yourself like the business you are, and never underestimate the power of professionalism. Understand the economics of this space, focus on creating real value, and keep pushing forward with intention. The world of content creation is wide open, and your professionalism is what's going to set you apart from the rest.

You've got the talent. Now go show the world you've got the business chops to match.

CHAPTER 8

FINANCIAL
MANAGEMENT FOR
CREATORS

Alright, creators, let's talk about money—not just how to make it, but how to keep it, grow it, and plan for your future. You've probably heard the saying, "It's not about how much you make; it's about how much you keep." And that couldn't be truer for creators like us. Whether you're raking in cash from brand deals, affiliate marketing, or your own products, managing your money is the key to building a sustainable career and securing your financial future.

The creator economy can be unpredictable. One month you're flush with cash from a viral video, and the next, things slow down. That's why it's crucial to get a handle on your finances—budget wisely, invest smartly, and plan for the future. Because at the end of the day, it's not just about today's paycheck; it's about setting yourself up for long-term success. Let's dive into some practical strategies to help you manage your money like a pro.

Importance of Financial Planning: Budgeting Basics for Creators

Let's start with the basics: financial planning. As a creator, your income might not look like a traditional 9-to-5 paycheck. It could come in waves, with big payouts from brand deals one month and quieter periods the next. That's why having a solid financial plan is essential—it gives you control, helps you manage the ups and downs, and ensures you're not living paycheck to paycheck.

1. Understanding Your Income Streams

The first step in financial planning is understanding where your money comes from. As a creator, you might have multiple income streams—ad revenue, sponsorships, product sales, affiliate commissions, and more. The goal is to get a clear picture of your monthly income, so you can plan your expenses accordingly.

Action Step: List out all your income sources and average out your monthly earnings. This will give you a baseline for your budget. Remember, it's okay if your income fluctuates—what's important is knowing your average and planning for those variations.

2. Create a Budget That Works for You

Budgeting doesn't have to be boring or restrictive—it's just a way to make sure your money is working for you. Think of it as your financial blueprint, guiding you on where to spend, save, and invest. Here's how to get started:

- **Track Your Spending:** Start by tracking every dollar you spend for a month. You can use apps like Mint, YNAB (You Need A Budget), or even a simple spreadsheet. Knowing where your money goes is the first step to controlling it.
- **Separate Business and Personal Finances:** As a creator, it's easy for your personal and business expenses to blur. Open separate bank accounts—one for business and one for personal. This makes it easier to track expenses, manage taxes, and see exactly what your business is costing you.
- **Allocate Your Income:** Use the 50/30/20 rule as a starting point: 50% of your income goes to needs (rent, bills, groceries), 30% to wants (eating out, entertainment), and 20% to savings and investments. Adjust these percentages based on your lifestyle and goals.

3. Plan for Irregular Income

Unlike a salaried job, your income as a creator can be inconsistent. To avoid the stress of not knowing if you'll have enough for the month, set aside a portion of your earnings during the good months to cover the slower ones. This is called a "buffer fund," and it's a lifesaver when cash flow isn't steady.

Action Step: Aim to save at least 3-6 months' worth of living expenses in your buffer fund. This safety net will give you peace of mind and the flexibility to say no to low-paying gigs that aren't worth your time.

4. Budget for Business Expenses

Being a creator comes with its own set of business expenses—gear, software, website hosting, advertising, and more. It's important to budget for these costs so you're not caught off guard. Regularly review your subscriptions and tools to make sure you're not paying for things you don't use.

Action Step: List all your recurring business expenses and set aside a portion of your income each month to cover them. If you have one-off costs like a new camera or editing software, plan for those in advance so they don't blow up your budget.

5. Don't Forget About Taxes

Taxes can be a rude awakening for creators, especially if you're not used to handling them on your own. Unlike a traditional job, where taxes are automatically deducted from your paycheck, creators are responsible for setting aside their own tax payments. The last thing you want is a surprise tax bill that you're not prepared for.

Action Step: Set aside at least 20-30% of your income for taxes, depending on your tax bracket and location. Use a separate savings account for your tax money so you're not tempted to dip into it. Consider working with an accountant who understands the creator economy to help you maximize deductions and stay compliant.

Building a Money Mindset: Moving from Scarcity to Abundance

Managing money isn't just about numbers—it's about mindset. As creators, we often start out hustling hard, scraping by, and doing whatever it takes to get ahead. But that scarcity mindset—thinking there's never enough, fearing that your next check will be your last—can hold you back from real financial growth. To thrive as a creator, you need to shift from scarcity to abundance. Here's how.

1. Recognize Your Money Stories

We all have money stories—beliefs and attitudes about money that we've picked up from our upbringing, experiences, and society. Maybe you grew up hearing "money doesn't grow on trees," or maybe you've struggled financially and believe you'll never have enough. These stories shape how you handle money, often without you even realizing it.

Action Step: Take some time to reflect on your money stories. What beliefs are you carrying that might be holding you back? Write them down, and then challenge them. For example, if you believe "I'll never be good with money," reframe it to "I'm learning to manage my money better every day."

2. Embrace an Abundance Mindset

An abundance mindset is about believing that there's enough for everyone and that you have the ability to create more wealth. It's knowing that opportunities are out there, and that your worth isn't tied to your current bank balance.

One of the best ways to cultivate an abundance mindset is to focus on gratitude and celebrate small wins. Did you land a new brand deal? Great! Did you hit your savings goal for the month? Awesome! These moments are proof that you're moving in the right direction, and they help reinforce the belief that more is possible.

Action Step: Start a gratitude journal specifically for your finances. Each week, write down three money wins, big or small. This simple habit helps you focus on the positive and shift your mindset from scarcity to abundance.

3. Set Financial Goals That Excite You

It's hard to stay motivated about saving money if you don't have a clear goal in mind. That's why it's essential to set financial goals that excite and inspire you. These goals should be personal, meaningful, and aligned with your values. Maybe it's saving up for your dream camera, paying off debt, or investing in a new course to level up your skills.

Action Step: Set short-term, mid-term, and long-term financial goals. Break them down into actionable steps and track your progress. The more specific your goals, the easier they'll be to achieve.

4. Invest in Yourself

Investing in yourself is one of the best ways to build an abundance mindset. This could mean investing in courses, attending workshops, hiring a coach, or upgrading your equipment. When you invest in yourself, you're betting on your future success—and that's the kind of mindset that attracts abundance.

Remember, investing in yourself doesn't always have to cost money. It could be time spent learning new skills, networking with other creators, or simply taking care of your mental and physical health.

5. Don't Be Afraid to Talk About Money

Money is often seen as a taboo topic, but talking about it openly can help break down the barriers of scarcity thinking. Connect with other creators, share your financial wins and challenges, and don't be afraid to ask for advice. The more we normalize conversations about money, the more empowered we become to take control of our financial futures.

Investing Early for Long-term Wealth: Stocks, Real Estate, and Beyond

One of the most powerful tools you have as a creator is the ability to invest your earnings. Investing isn't just for the wealthy—it's for anyone who wants to grow their money and build long-term wealth. The sooner you start, the more time your money has to grow, thanks to the magic of compound interest. Let's explore some of the most popular investment options and how you can get started.

1. Understanding the Power of Investing

Investing is all about making your money work for you. Instead of letting your cash sit in a savings account earning next to nothing, investing allows you to put your money into assets that can grow over time, like stocks, real estate, or even your own business.

The earlier you start investing, the more you benefit from compound interest—the process of earning returns on both your initial investment and the returns that accumulate over time. It's like a snowball effect, where your money grows exponentially the longer it's invested.

Action Step: Commit to starting your investment journey, even if it's with a small amount. You don't need to be rich to invest—just consistent. Even $50 a month can grow into something significant over time.

2. Investing in Stocks and ETFs

Stocks represent ownership in a company, and when you invest in stocks, you're buying a piece of that company. Exchange-traded funds (ETFs) are collections of stocks or bonds that you can buy as a single investment, offering diversification and lower risk.

How to Get Started with Stocks and ETFs:

- **Open a Brokerage Account:** Platforms like Robinhood, Vanguard, and Fidelity make it easy to start investing with little to no fees. Opening an account is quick, and you can start buying stocks or ETFs with as little as a few dollars.
- **Diversify Your Portfolio:** Don't put all your eggs in one basket. Spread your investments across different sectors and industries to reduce risk. ETFs are great for beginners because they offer built-in diversification.
- **Invest Consistently:** Set up automatic contributions to your investment account. Whether it's $50 a month or $500, consistency is key. Investing regularly, regardless of market conditions, is known as dollar-cost averaging, and it helps you build wealth over time.

3. Real Estate: Building Wealth with Property

Real estate is a popular investment option for creators who want to build long-term wealth. Owning property can provide rental income, tax benefits, and appreciation over time. You don't have to buy a house outright to get started—there are more accessible

THE CONTENT TO CASH BIBLE

options, like REITs (real estate investment trusts) that let you invest in real estate without owning physical property.

How to Get Started with Real Estate:

- **Save for a Down Payment:** If you're interested in buying property, start saving for a down payment. The more you can put down upfront, the better your financing options will be.
- **Consider House Hacking:** House hacking is a strategy where you buy a multi-unit property, live in one unit, and rent out the others. The rental income can cover your mortgage, allowing you to live for free while building equity.
- **Invest in REITs:** If buying property isn't feasible, consider REITs, which are companies that own, operate, or finance income-producing real estate. You can buy shares of REITs just like you would stocks, gaining exposure to real estate without the hassle of being a landlord.

4. Invest in Your Own Business

As a creator, your brand is your business, and investing in it can yield huge returns. This might mean upgrading your equipment, hiring a team member to help with editing, or launching a new product line. The money you put back into your business is an investment in your growth and future success.

Action Step: Look at your business expenses as investments. What can you do to improve your content, streamline your workflow, or increase your revenue? Make strategic decisions that help you grow and scale.

5. Consider Alternative Investments

Beyond stocks and real estate, there are alternative investments that can diversify your portfolio even further. This includes options like peer-to-peer lending, investing in art or collectibles, or even cryptocurrency. While these investments can carry more risk, they also offer the potential for high returns.

How to Approach Alternative Investments:

- **Do Your Research:** Alternative investments aren't for everyone, and they often come with higher risk. Make sure you understand what you're getting into and how it fits into your overall investment strategy.
- **Start Small:** If you're curious about alternative investments, start with a small amount that you're comfortable losing. Test the waters and learn as you go.
- **Stay Diversified:** Keep alternative investments as a small part of your overall portfolio. The bulk of your investments should still be in traditional assets like stocks, bonds, or real estate.

Creating Your Own Retirement Plan: Because Creators Need Security Too

Let's be real—most creators aren't thinking about retirement when they're busy building their brand. But here's the thing: retirement planning isn't just for people with corporate jobs. As a creator, you need a plan for the future, because there's no pension, 401(k), or company-sponsored retirement fund waiting for you.

Creating your own retirement plan gives you the security of knowing that you're building a nest egg for your future. It's about setting yourself up to enjoy life on your terms, even when the brand deals slow down.

1. Open a Retirement Account

The first step in creating your retirement plan is opening an account designed for long-term savings. There are several options available, even if you're self-employed:

- **Roth IRA:** A Roth IRA is a great option for creators because contributions are made with after-tax dollars, meaning your money grows tax-free, and withdrawals in retirement are also tax-free. There are income limits, so check if you qualify.
- **Traditional IRA:** Contributions to a traditional IRA may be tax-deductible, which can lower your taxable

income for the year. However, withdrawals in retirement are taxed as regular income.

- **Solo 401(k):** A Solo 401(k) is designed for self-employed individuals and offers higher contribution limits than an IRA. You can contribute as both the employee and employer, allowing you to save more aggressively for retirement.

2. Automate Your Contributions

One of the best ways to stay on track with retirement savings is to automate your contributions. Set up automatic transfers from your bank account to your retirement account each month. This makes saving a habit and removes the temptation to skip contributions.

Action Step: Start with what you can afford, even if it's just $100 a month. The important thing is to start. You can always increase your contributions as your income grows.

3. Invest for Growth

The money in your retirement account shouldn't just sit in cash—it needs to be invested to grow. Most retirement accounts offer a range of investment options, from stocks and bonds to mutual funds and ETFs. Choose a diversified mix that aligns with your risk tolerance and time horizon.

Action Step: If you're not sure where to start, consider a target-date fund, which automatically adjusts the investment mix as you approach retirement. Or consult a financial advisor who can help you create a personalized investment strategy.

4. Plan for Healthcare Costs

Healthcare is one of the biggest expenses in retirement, and it's often overlooked. As a creator, you won't have employer-sponsored health insurance, so it's essential to factor healthcare costs into your retirement plan.

Consider opening a Health Savings Account (HSA) if you have a high-deductible health plan. HSAs offer triple tax benefits: contributions are tax-deductible, the money grows tax-free, and withdrawals for qualified medical expenses are also tax-free. Plus, after age 65, you can use HSA funds for non-medical expenses without penalties.

5. Protect Your Retirement with Insurance

Insurance isn't the most exciting topic, but it's a crucial part of protecting your retirement savings. Consider disability insurance, which provides income if you're unable to work due to illness or injury. Life insurance is also important, especially if you have dependents who rely on your income.

Action Step: Review your insurance needs annually and make sure you have adequate coverage. The right insurance can prevent a financial setback from derailing your retirement plans.

Wrapping It All Up: Your Financial Future as a Creator

Financial management might not be the sexiest part of being a creator, but it's one of the most important. By budgeting wisely, investing early, and planning for retirement, you're not just making money—you're building a legacy. The creator economy offers endless opportunities, but with those opportunities comes the responsibility to manage your money well.

Remember, financial freedom isn't just about how much you earn; it's about how you manage, invest, and plan for the future. Take control of your finances today, so you can enjoy the freedom and security of a well-managed financial future tomorrow.

You've got the talent, the audience, and the drive. Now, let's make sure you've got the financial foundation to support your journey, both now and for years to come.

CHAPTER 9

LIFE INSURANCE AND FINANCIAL SECURITY

Alright, creators, let's dive into something we all know we need to think about, but most of us keep putting off—life insurance and financial security. Yeah, I know, it's not the most exciting topic. You'd probably rather be talking about your next big content idea or a new way to engage your audience. But here's the truth: part of being a successful creator isn't just about living your best life today, but also making sure you and your loved ones are protected for tomorrow.

We're going to get into why life insurance isn't just something for "other people" or just for when you're older. It's for right now, especially if you're a creator who's self-employed, relies on variable income, and doesn't have a traditional safety net. This chapter will break down the basics of life insurance, help you choose the right policy, and guide you through planning for the unexpected so you can keep your legacy intact. Let's get started.

Understanding Life Insurance Options for Creators

Life insurance might seem like a boring, complicated topic that's easy to push aside, but understanding your options can make a world of difference for your peace of mind—and your family's financial future. The main goal of life insurance is to provide financial support to your loved ones if something were to happen to you. It's a way of ensuring that your hard work, income, and legacy are protected, even if life takes an unexpected turn.

But let's be real—life insurance isn't just a "one-size-fits-all" deal. There are different types of policies, each with its pros and cons, and it's important to know what you're signing up for. Let's break down the main types of life insurance so you can understand what might work best for you.

1. Term Life Insurance: The No-Frills, Affordable Option

Term life insurance is the most straightforward and affordable type of life insurance, which makes it a popular choice, especially for younger people and those just starting to think about financial security. With a term policy, you're covered for a specific period—usually 10, 20, or 30 years. If you pass away during that term, your beneficiaries receive a payout, known as the death benefit. If you outlive the term, the policy simply ends, and there's no cash value left behind.

Pros of Term Life Insurance:

- **Affordable Premiums:** Term life is typically the least expensive option because it's purely insurance—there's no investment component or cash value. This makes it accessible for most people, especially if you're on a budget.
- **Simple and Easy to Understand:** There aren't a lot of bells and whistles with term life insurance, making it easy to understand exactly what you're getting.
- **Flexible Terms:** You can choose a term length that suits your needs. For example, a 20-year term can cover you until your kids are grown or until your mortgage is paid off.

Cons of Term Life Insurance:

1. **No Cash Value:** Term life insurance doesn't build cash value, so if you outlive the policy, there's no payout or refund of premiums.
2. **Rates Increase with Age:** If you decide to renew or buy a new policy later in life, the premiums will be higher because insurance rates increase with age.

Who Is Term Life Insurance For? Term life is great for creators who want affordable coverage to protect their family during critical years—like when you're raising kids, paying off debt, or building your business. It's an ideal choice if you're looking for straightforward protection without the higher costs of permanent insurance.

2. Whole Life Insurance: Coverage for Life with a Savings Component

Whole life insurance is a type of permanent life insurance, meaning it covers you for your entire life as long as you continue paying the premiums. In addition to providing a death benefit, whole life insurance also builds cash value over time. This cash value grows tax-deferred and can be borrowed against or withdrawn, providing a financial cushion you can use while you're still alive.

Pros of Whole Life Insurance:

- **Lifetime Coverage:** Whole life insurance covers you for life, which means your beneficiaries will receive a payout no matter when you pass away, as long as the policy is active.
- **Cash Value Component:** Part of your premium goes toward building cash value, which you can access through loans or withdrawals. This can be useful for financial emergencies, supplementing retirement income, or even funding major expenses.
- **Fixed Premiums:** Premiums are usually fixed for the life of the policy, so you won't see rate increases as you age.

Cons of Whole Life Insurance:

- **Higher Premiums:** Whole life insurance is significantly more expensive than term insurance because it combines coverage with a savings component. You're paying for both insurance and investment.

- **Complexity:** Whole life policies can be complicated with various fees, terms, and conditions. It's important to fully understand the policy before buying.

Who Is Whole Life Insurance For? Whole life insurance is a good option if you're looking for lifetime coverage and are willing to pay higher premiums in exchange for building cash value. It's ideal for those who want a combination of insurance and a savings component or who are interested in using life insurance as a financial planning tool.

3. Universal Life Insurance: Flexibility with Investment Potential

Universal life insurance is another type of permanent life insurance, but it offers more flexibility than whole life. You can adjust your premiums and death benefits within certain limits, and like whole life, it builds cash value. Some universal life policies even allow you to invest the cash value in various sub-accounts, similar to mutual funds.

Pros of Universal Life Insurance:

- **Flexible Premiums:** You can adjust your premium payments (within policy limits) based on your financial situation. This flexibility can be appealing if your income fluctuates.

- **Cash Value Growth:** The cash value grows tax-deferred and can be used for loans or withdrawals, providing a potential source of income.
- **Adjustable Death Benefit:** You can increase or decrease your death benefit, depending on your needs, which isn't possible with other types of insurance.

Cons of Universal Life Insurance:

- **Market Risk:** If you choose a policy with investment options, your cash value growth is tied to market performance, which means there's a risk of losing money.
- **Complex Structure:** Universal life insurance can be complex, with fees, investment risks, and terms that require careful management.

Who Is Universal Life Insurance For? Universal life insurance is a good choice if you're looking for permanent coverage with the added flexibility to adjust your premiums and death benefit. It's suited for creators who want more control over their policy and are comfortable managing the investment aspect.

Choosing the Right Policy: Protecting Your Income and Legacy

Now that you know the basics, it's time to figure out which life insurance policy is right for you. The decision ultimately comes down to your financial goals, current needs, and long-term plans.

Here are some steps to help you choose the best policy for your situation.

1. Assess Your Financial Needs

The first step in choosing the right life insurance policy is understanding your financial needs. Ask yourself: What do you want your life insurance to cover? Is it to replace your income, pay off debts, cover your children's education, or leave a legacy? Knowing your primary goals will help you determine the amount of coverage you need.

Action Step: Use an online life insurance calculator to estimate how much coverage is right for you based on your financial obligations, income, and long-term goals. This will give you a solid starting point when comparing policies.

2. Consider Your Budget

Your budget plays a big role in deciding which type of life insurance to buy. Term life is typically more affordable, making it a good choice if you need coverage but are on a tighter budget. If you're in a position to invest more and want a policy that builds cash value, whole or universal life might be worth considering.

Action Step: Look at your monthly budget and see what you can comfortably afford to spend on life insurance. Remember, it's better to have some coverage than none at all, so don't let the cost deter you from getting protected.

3. Evaluate the Policy Terms

Every life insurance policy comes with its own set of terms and conditions. Pay close attention to these details, especially the fine print regarding premiums, payout conditions, and any potential exclusions. For example, some policies have waiting periods before coverage kicks in fully, or they may exclude certain causes of death.

Action Step: Ask your insurance agent or provider to explain any terms you don't understand. Don't sign anything until you're completely clear on what you're getting and what it will cost over the life of the policy.

4. Think About Your Future Needs

Life isn't static—your needs, income, and goals will evolve over time. When choosing a policy, consider how your needs might change. If you're young and just starting out, a term policy might make sense now, but be open to revisiting your options as your financial situation improves.

Action Step: Schedule a yearly review of your life insurance coverage. As your life changes—marriage, kids, buying a home, growing your business—your insurance needs will change too.

5. Work with a Financial Advisor

Navigating life insurance can be confusing, especially with so many options on the table. A financial advisor or insurance agent can help you compare policies, explain the benefits and drawbacks, and guide you toward the best decision for your unique situation.

Action Step: Find a financial advisor who understands the creator economy. They can provide personalized advice based on your income, lifestyle, and future plans.

Ensuring Long-term Financial Security: Planning for the Unexpected

Life insurance is just one piece of the financial security puzzle. Ensuring long-term security means planning for the unexpected—protecting your income, managing risks, and having a backup plan in place. Let's explore some strategies to help you stay financially secure, no matter what life throws your way.

1. Emergency Fund: Your First Line of Defense

Before anything else, your first priority should be building an emergency fund. This is your safety net, designed to cover unexpected expenses like medical bills, car repairs, or a sudden loss of income. A well-funded emergency fund prevents you from dipping into your investments or going into debt when life doesn't go as planned.

Action Step: Aim to save at least 3-6 months' worth of living expenses in a separate, easily accessible savings account. Start small and contribute regularly until you reach your goal.

2. Disability Insurance: Protecting Your Income

Disability insurance is often overlooked, but it's crucial—especially for creators who rely on their health and ability to work to earn a living. Disability insurance provides income if you're unable to work due to illness or injury. It's like having a paycheck backup plan that keeps you financially afloat when life throws a curveball.

Action Step: Look into disability insurance options, either through private insurers or professional associations that offer group rates. Assess the coverage amount and duration to ensure it meets your needs.

3. Health Insurance: Don't Skimp on Coverage

Health insurance isn't just a nice-to-have; it's a must. Medical expenses can quickly spiral out of control, and without insurance, you're left paying out-of-pocket, which can drain your savings and derail your financial goals. Even if you're young and healthy, unexpected accidents or illnesses can happen to anyone.

Action Step: Explore health insurance options through the marketplace, professional associations, or even a partner's employer plan if available. Choose a plan that balances premium costs with coverage benefits to protect your health and your wallet.

4. Create a Will and Estate Plan

Estate planning isn't just for the wealthy—it's for anyone who wants to ensure their assets are distributed according to their wishes. A will outlines who gets what when you pass away, while other estate planning tools like trusts can help minimize taxes and protect your assets for future generations.

Action Step: Draft a basic will that includes your assets, beneficiaries, and any specific instructions you have for your estate. As your wealth grows, consider working with an estate attorney to create a more comprehensive plan.

5. Regularly Review Your Financial Plan

Life happens, and your financial needs change. That's why it's important to regularly review and update your financial plan, including your life insurance and other coverage. What worked last year might not be enough this year, especially as your business grows, your family expands, or your financial goals evolve.

Action Step: Schedule a financial check-up at least once a year. Review your insurance policies, update your beneficiaries, and assess whether your current coverage still meets your needs.

Wrapping It All Up: Securing Your Future as a Creator

Navigating life insurance and financial security can feel daunting, but it's an essential part of being a responsible creator. It's about more than just protecting your income today—it's about safeguarding your legacy and ensuring that the people you care about are taken care of, no matter what.

Remember, you're not just building a brand or chasing the next big opportunity; you're building a life. Life insurance, emergency funds, and financial planning aren't just for "other people." They're for you, too. Taking the time to plan now means that you're not just prepared for the best moments of your journey—you're ready for the challenges, too.

So take control of your financial future. Understand your options, choose the right coverage, and make sure you're protected. Your peace of mind, your loved ones, and your legacy are worth it.

Now, let's secure that bag for the long haul.

CHAPTER 10

SUSTAINING LONG-TERM GROWTH

Alright, creators, you've built your brand, grown your audience, and started making money from your influence. But now comes the real challenge: sustaining that growth for the long haul. The creator economy moves fast, and staying relevant means continuously evolving, expanding, and finding new ways to connect with your audience.

If you're in this for the long game—and I know you are—you've got to think beyond the next post, the next video, or the next viral trend. This chapter is all about developing a long-term growth strategy that will keep you thriving not just today, but years down the line. We'll dive into how to scale beyond social media, expand your influence through books, courses, and speaking engagements, diversify your income streams, and, most importantly, take care of your mental health along the way. Let's get into it.

Developing a Long-term Growth Strategy: Scaling Beyond Social Media

Social media is a powerful tool, no doubt. It's where you connect with your audience, share your message, and build your brand. But if your entire business is dependent on algorithms, trends, and platforms you don't control, you're putting your future at risk. Remember when Instagram crashed for a few hours, and everyone freaked out? That's why you need a plan that scales beyond social media.

To sustain long-term growth, you need to think about how to turn your influence into a business that can weather changes in the social media landscape. Here's how to get started:

1. Treat Your Brand Like a Business

If you're still treating your content like a side hustle or a hobby, it's time to shift your mindset. You're not just a creator—you're a business owner. That means developing a business plan, setting goals, and thinking strategically about your next moves.

Action Step: Start with a simple business plan. Outline your vision, mission, and values. Identify your target audience, income streams, and goals for the next year, three years, and five years. This doesn't have to be a rigid document, but having a clear roadmap will help guide your decisions.

2. Build an Owned Audience

Social media platforms are great, but they're rented space. The algorithm changes, platform policies shift, and suddenly, your reach is cut in half. That's why it's crucial to build an owned audience—people you can connect with directly, no matter what happens on social media.

How to Build an Owned Audience:

- **Email List:** Your email list is one of your most valuable assets because it's yours. Use lead magnets like free e-books, templates, or exclusive content to encourage sign-ups. Regularly engage with your subscribers through newsletters, updates, and value-packed content.
- **Website and Blog:** Your website is your digital home base. It's where people can learn more about you, find your content, and even make purchases. A blog adds value and boosts your SEO, making it easier for new people to discover you.
- **Community Platforms:** Consider creating a private community on platforms like Discord, Slack, or Mighty Networks. This gives your audience a space to connect with you and each other, beyond the noise of social media.

3. Set SMART Goals

Growing for the sake of growing isn't sustainable. You need specific, measurable, achievable, relevant, and time-bound (SMART) goals to keep you focused and on track. Whether it's launching a new product, hitting a revenue target, or expanding your brand into new areas, clear goals help you stay aligned with your long-term vision.

Action Step: Break down your big goals into smaller, actionable steps. If your goal is to launch an online course, start by outlining the curriculum, creating a content calendar, and setting deadlines for each module. Track your progress and adjust as needed.

4. Invest in Systems and Automation

As you grow, you'll quickly realize that doing everything manually isn't sustainable. Investing in systems and automation tools can save you time, reduce stress, and allow you to focus on what you do best—creating.

Automation Ideas for Creators:

1. **Content Scheduling:** Use tools like Later, Buffer, or Hootsuite to schedule your social media posts in advance. This keeps your content consistent without you having to be glued to your phone.

2. **Email Marketing:** Set up automated email sequences to welcome new subscribers, nurture leads, or promote your products. Platforms like ConvertKit, Mailchimp, or ActiveCampaign make this easy to manage.

3. **Project Management:** Tools like Asana, Trello, or Notion help you keep track of tasks, collaborate with your team, and streamline your workflow.

5. Embrace Continuous Learning

The creator economy is constantly evolving, and what worked last year might not work today. To sustain growth, you need to be a life-long learner. Stay curious, keep experimenting, and don't be afraid to pivot when something isn't working.

Action Step: Invest in your education. Take courses, attend webinars, read books, and network with other creators. Staying up-to-date with industry trends and new technologies will keep you ahead of the curve.

Expanding Influence Beyond Social Media: Books, Courses, and Speaking Engagements

To truly build a lasting brand, you need to expand your influence beyond social media. It's about leveraging your expertise, sharing your story, and positioning yourself as a thought leader in your niche. Let's explore some of the most effective ways to do that.

1. Write a Book: Share Your Expertise

Writing a book is one of the most powerful ways to establish credibility and reach a wider audience. A book isn't just a product; it's a legacy piece that positions you as an authority in your field. Plus, it opens doors to new opportunities like speaking engagements, media appearances, and consulting gigs.

How to Get Started with Writing a Book:

- **Define Your Purpose:** What do you want your book to accomplish? Is it to educate, inspire, entertain, or establish your expertise? Having a clear purpose will guide your writing process.
- **Outline Your Content:** Start with an outline of your main points, chapters, and key takeaways. This will help you stay organized and focused as you write.
- **Choose Your Publishing Route:** Decide whether you want to self-publish or pursue a traditional publishing deal. Self-publishing offers more control and faster timelines, while traditional publishing provides wider distribution and credibility.

Action Step: Set a writing schedule and stick to it. Even if you're writing just a few hundred words a day, consistency adds up. Before you know it, you'll have a complete manuscript.

2. Create Online Courses: Teach What You Know

Online courses are a fantastic way to monetize your expertise while providing value to your audience. They allow you to package your knowledge into a structured format that people can access anytime, anywhere. Courses also offer the potential for passive income—you create it once, and it keeps generating revenue.

How to Create a Successful Online Course:

- **Identify a Topic that Resonates:** What does your audience consistently ask you about? What problems can you solve? The best course topics come directly from your audience's needs.

- **Structure Your Content:** Break down your course into modules and lessons, and create a clear learning path for your students. Use a mix of videos, worksheets, and quizzes to keep the content engaging.

- **Choose a Platform:** Platforms like Teachable, Thinkific, or Kajabi make it easy to host, sell, and market your course. They handle the tech side, so you can focus on delivering great content.

Action Step: Validate your course idea before investing too much time and money. Offer a free webinar or mini-course to gauge interest and collect feedback. If the response is positive, move forward with creating the full course.

3. Speaking Engagements: Share Your Message on Stage

Speaking engagements are another powerful way to expand your influence and connect with your audience on a deeper level. Whether it's keynoting at conferences, hosting workshops, or participating in panels, public speaking positions you as a leader in your field and often leads to new opportunities.

How to Get Started with Speaking Engagements:

- **Build Your Speaker Profile:** Create a speaker page on your website with your bio, topics you cover, and testimonials from past events. Include video clips of you speaking if you have them—it's the best way to showcase your style and presence.

- **Pitch Yourself:** Don't wait for invitations to come to you. Reach out to event organizers, podcasts, or local groups that align with your message. Pitch yourself as a speaker and explain what value you can bring to their audience.

- **Hone Your Speaking Skills:** Public speaking can be nerve-wracking, but practice makes perfect. Join a group like Toastmasters, take an online speaking course, or simply practice in front of a mirror. The more you do it, the more confident you'll become.

Action Step: Start small if needed. Offer to speak at local meet-ups, host a free workshop, or do virtual talks on Instagram Live or Zoom. The more you put yourself out there, the more comfortable and skilled you'll become.

Diversifying Income Streams: Beyond Ads and Sponsorships

Relying solely on ads and sponsorships can leave you vulnerable. If one income stream dries up, you could find yourself scrambling.

That's why diversifying your income is critical for long-term growth. Here are some creative ways to expand your revenue sources.

1. Offer Coaching or Consulting

If you have expertise that others can benefit from, consider offering one-on-one coaching or consulting services. This can be particularly valuable if you're an expert in a specific niche, like business strategy, social media growth, or mindset coaching.

How to Get Started with Coaching or Consulting:

- **Define Your Offer:** Be clear about what you're offering and who it's for. What specific problem can you help people solve? Define your packages, pricing, and process.
- **Create a Sales Funnel:** Use your social media and website to drive traffic to your coaching or consulting services. Offer free resources like guides, webinars, or mini-sessions to build trust and attract potential clients.
- **Leverage Testimonials:** Testimonials from satisfied clients are gold. They build social proof and help potential clients feel confident in investing in your services.

Action Step: Offer a few free or discounted sessions in exchange for honest feedback and testimonials. Use this feedback to refine your offer and boost your marketing materials.

2. Sell Digital Products

Digital products like e-books, templates, presets, or digital downloads are a great way to earn passive income while providing value to your audience. Once created, they require little maintenance and can be sold repeatedly.

Ideas for Digital Products:

- **E-books or Guides:** Share your expertise in a downloadable format that's easy to sell directly from your website or platforms like Gumroad.
- **Templates and Tools:** Create templates for social media posts, spreadsheets, planners, or any other tools that your audience would find helpful.
- **Digital Art or Printables:** If you're a creative, consider selling digital art prints, illustrations, or printable planners. These products are easy to create and deliver instantly.

Action Step: Use Canva, InDesign, or other design tools to create your digital products. Set up an online shop using Etsy, Shopify, or your own website to start selling.

3. Licensing Your Content

Licensing your content means allowing others to use your work in exchange for a fee. This could be photos, videos, graphics, or even music that brands or individuals can use for their own projects. Licensing is a great way to earn money from content you've already created.

How to Start Licensing Your Content:

- **Join Licensing Platforms:** Sites like Shutterstock, Adobe Stock, and Getty Images allow creators to upload and sell their work for use by others. You earn royalties every time someone purchases your content.

- **Create Your Own Licensing Agreement:** If you prefer to license directly, you can create your own licensing agreements and work with brands or individuals who want to use your content.

Action Step: Start by uploading some of your best work to a licensing platform and see how it performs. Experiment with different types of content to find out what sells best.

Building Resilience: Managing Mental Health and Avoiding Burnout

Let's get real for a second: being a creator is demanding. The pressure to constantly create, stay relevant, and keep up with the ever-changing landscape can take a toll on your mental health. If you're not careful, burnout can creep up and derail everything you've worked so hard to build. Building resilience isn't just a nice-to-have—it's essential for sustaining long-term growth.

1. Set Boundaries: Protect Your Time and Energy

One of the biggest challenges creators face is the pressure to always be "on." The truth is, you don't have to be available 24/7. Setting boundaries around your work time, social media use, and personal life is key to maintaining your mental health.

Action Step: Define your work hours and stick to them. Schedule regular breaks throughout your day, and take at least one full day off each week to recharge. Communicate your boundaries clearly with your audience if needed—they'll respect you for it.

2. Prioritize Self-Care

Self-care isn't just about bubble baths and spa days (though those are great, too). It's about taking care of your physical, mental, and emotional well-being. This might mean exercising regularly, eating nutritious food, getting enough sleep, and setting aside time to unwind.

Action Step: Schedule self-care into your calendar like you would a meeting or a content deadline. Whether it's a daily walk, journaling, meditation, or simply reading a book, make self-care a non-negotiable part of your routine.

3. Learn to Say No

Not every opportunity is worth your time, and saying yes to everything can lead to overwhelm and burnout. Learning to say no—whether it's to a brand deal that doesn't align with your values or a project that doesn't excite you—is a powerful form of self-care.

Action Step: When faced with a new opportunity, ask yourself: Does this align with my goals? Does it excite me? Will it add unnecessary stress? If the answer is no, give yourself permission to turn it down.

4. Seek Support When You Need It

You don't have to do it all alone. If you're feeling overwhelmed, anxious, or burned out, seek support from others. This could be talking to a friend, joining a creator community, or working with a therapist or coach who understands the unique challenges of the creator economy.

Action Step: Build a support network. Surround yourself with people who understand your journey and can offer encouragement, advice, or simply a listening ear when you need it.

5. Focus on Progress, Not Perfection

Perfectionism is a trap that many creators fall into, and it's one of the biggest contributors to burnout. Remember that done is better than perfect. Your audience doesn't expect you to be flawless—they just want you to show up authentically.

Action Step: Set realistic expectations for yourself and celebrate small wins. Progress, no matter how small, is still progress. Let go of the pressure to be perfect and focus on moving forward.

Wrapping It All Up: Growing for the Long Haul

Sustaining long-term growth as a creator is about more than just staying relevant—it's about building a resilient brand, diversifying your income, and taking care of yourself along the way. The creator economy offers incredible opportunities, but it also demands that you think strategically, stay adaptable, and prioritize your well-being.

Remember, you're in control of your growth. By expanding your influence beyond social media, diversifying your income streams, and building resilience, you're setting yourself up for a thriving, sustainable career. So take a deep breath, keep learning, keep creating, and keep taking care of yourself.

The future is yours, and it's looking bright.

CHAPTER 11

CASE STUDIES AND
SUCCESS STORIES

A lright, creators, we've covered the strategies, the mindset shifts, and the nitty-gritty of growing and sustaining your brand. But let's be real—sometimes, nothing beats hearing real-life stories from people who've been in the trenches, hustled through the highs and lows, and come out on top. This chapter is all about learning from those who've walked the path before you, taking their wins, losses, and lessons, and using them to fuel your journey.

We're diving into case studies and success stories from some of the most inspiring creators in the game. These are the people who have turned their passions into profitable, sustainable careers—through grit, creativity, and a whole lot of hard work. From YouTube stars and Instagram influencers to podcasters, authors, and entrepreneurs, these creators share what they did right, the mistakes they learned from, and the real talk about what it takes to make it in the creator economy.

So grab your notebook, because there's a lot to unpack here. Let's get into it.

Interviews with Successful Creators: What They Did Right

1. The Story of Marie Kondo: Sparking Joy and Building a Global Brand

Marie Kondo is a name synonymous with organization and minimalism. She's the author of the best-selling book *The Life-Changing Magic of Tidying Up*, host of the hit Netflix show *Tidying Up with Marie Kondo*, and the founder of KonMari, a lifestyle brand that's built around her unique philosophy of decluttering and sparking joy. But Marie's journey didn't happen overnight—it was a combination of passion, strategic branding, and the ability to tap into a global need for simplicity.

What She Did Right:

- **Niche Mastery:** Marie didn't just stumble into the world of tidying up; she mastered it. She started her organizing business in Japan as a teenager and spent years refining her method before sharing it with the world. She identified a niche that resonated deeply with people—organization as a form of self-care and mental clarity—and owned it.
- **Consistent Branding:** From her book to her show to her social media presence, Marie's brand is consistent.

The calm, joyful, and minimalist aesthetic runs through everything she does, making her instantly recognizable. She doesn't just sell a product; she sells a lifestyle.

- **Leveraging Multiple Platforms:** Marie didn't limit herself to one platform. She started with a book, expanded to a TV show, and then launched an entire brand with products, courses, and a certification program. This multi-platform approach allowed her to reach a broad audience and build multiple revenue streams.

Key Takeaway: Master your niche and stay true to your brand. Consistency builds trust, and when people know what to expect from you, they keep coming back for more.

2. The Rise of MrBeast: YouTube's King of Viral Content and Philanthropy

Jimmy Donaldson, better known as MrBeast, is a YouTube sensation known for his over-the-top stunts, viral challenges, and massive giveaways. With over 100 million subscribers, MrBeast didn't just become famous by chance—he's a master strategist who knows how to create content that grabs attention and keeps viewers hooked.

What He Did Right:

1. **Reinvesting in Content:** From the very beginning, MrBeast reinvested almost all his earnings back into his content. His videos started with modest budgets, but as

he made more money, he spent more—upping the stakes, the production quality, and the entertainment value. This reinvestment strategy allowed him to scale his content to levels that no one else was doing.

2. **Audience Engagement:** MrBeast understands his audience better than anyone. He's not just creating videos; he's creating experiences. Whether it's giving away millions of dollars, organizing elaborate challenges, or launching his own burger chain, MrBeast always keeps his audience at the center of everything he does.

3. **Diversifying Revenue Streams:** Beyond YouTube ad revenue, MrBeast has expanded into other areas—launching merchandise, creating his own food brand (MrBeast Burger), and exploring philanthropy through massive giveaways and charitable donations. This diversification not only boosts his income but also solidifies his brand as one that's bigger than just YouTube.

Key Takeaway: Don't be afraid to reinvest in yourself and your content. Sometimes, the biggest risks yield the biggest rewards. And always remember that your audience is your most valuable asset—keep them engaged and involved in your journey.

3. The Transformation of Jenna Kutcher: From Wedding Photographer to Business Mogul

Jenna Kutcher is a prime example of a creator who didn't just stick to one lane. Starting out as a wedding photographer, Jenna built a six-figure business and then pivoted to teaching others how to do the same. Today, she's a successful entrepreneur, podcast host, and author who empowers women to live authentically and build profitable businesses.

What She Did Right:

- **Pivoting with Purpose:** Jenna didn't wait until she was burned out to make a change. When she realized she wanted more than just a photography business, she pivoted to education—teaching others how to grow their brands, build marketing funnels, and create passive income streams. Her willingness to evolve with her interests has kept her business fresh and relevant.

- **Authenticity and Transparency:** Jenna's brand is built on being real. She shares her highs, her lows, and everything in between, allowing her audience to connect with her on a deeply personal level. This authenticity has created a loyal community that feels more like a supportive tribe than just followers.

- **Building a Brand Beyond Social Media:** Jenna didn't rely solely on Instagram to build her brand. She launched a successful podcast, created online courses, and wrote a book, all while maintaining her personal touch. By expanding her brand beyond social media, Jenna has built a business that's sustainable and diversified.

Key Takeaway: Don't be afraid to pivot when your passions evolve. Staying authentic and sharing your journey—both the good and the bad—creates a powerful connection with your audience.

Lessons Learned and Best Practices: Avoiding Common Pitfalls

Success doesn't come without its fair share of setbacks. Every creator who's made it big has stumbled, faced challenges, and learned valuable lessons along the way. Let's dig into some of the most common pitfalls and the best practices these successful creators have shared to help you avoid them.

1. Burnout is Real: Don't Ignore It

One of the biggest challenges creators face is burnout. The pressure to constantly produce content, keep up with trends, and stay engaged with your audience can be overwhelming. Many creators, including top YouTubers and influencers, have had to take breaks from their platforms to recharge. The lesson here? Burnout isn't a sign of weakness—it's a signal that you need to prioritize your well-being.

Best Practice: Set boundaries and stick to them. Schedule downtime, take regular breaks, and don't be afraid to step back when you need to. Your audience will still be there when you return, and they'll appreciate the honesty if you're transparent about needing a breather.

2. Don't Chase Trends at the Cost of Your Brand

It's tempting to jump on every viral trend, especially when it seems like everyone else is doing it. But chasing trends without considering how they fit into your brand can confuse your audience and dilute your message. Successful creators have learned to balance staying relevant with staying true to their core values.

Best Practice: Ask yourself if a trend aligns with your brand before jumping in. If it doesn't feel authentic, skip it. Focus on creating content that's true to you, even if it's not what everyone else is doing. Your unique voice is what sets you apart.

3. Diversify Early and Often

Relying on one platform or income stream is risky. Algorithms change, trends shift, and what works today might not work tomorrow. Many successful creators have faced this hard reality and learned the importance of diversification the hard way.

Best Practice: Don't wait until you hit a snag to start diversifying. Explore different platforms, revenue streams, and business models early on. Whether it's launching a product, starting a podcast, or creating a course, having multiple ways to generate income gives you stability and security.

4. Invest in Yourself and Your Team

Successful creators understand the value of investing in themselves and their teams. From upgrading equipment to hiring help, these investments can take your content—and your business—to the next level. Trying to do everything yourself isn't sustainable, and it often leads to burnout and missed opportunities.

Best Practice: Don't be afraid to spend money on tools, education, or team members that can help you grow. Hiring an editor, virtual assistant, or social media manager can free up your time to focus on what you do best—creating.

5. Keep Evolving: Adapt or Get Left Behind

The creator landscape is always changing. New platforms emerge, audience preferences shift, and the way we consume content evolves. Creators who have stood the test of time are the ones who've been willing to adapt, pivot, and reinvent themselves when necessary.

Best Practice: Stay curious and keep learning. Be willing to experiment with new formats, platforms, and ideas. The most successful creators are those who aren't afraid to change when the industry demands it.

Inspiration and Motivation for Aspiring Creators: Real Talk About the Grind

Let's get real about the journey, because being a creator isn't all brand deals, viral videos, and sponsorships. It's a grind, and it takes a level of resilience, creativity, and perseverance that not everyone is willing to commit to. But if you're reading this, you've already got the drive—you just need the motivation to keep pushing forward. Here's some real talk from successful creators about the ups, the downs, and why it's all worth it.

1. "Success Isn't Linear, and That's Okay." – Nabela Noor

Nabela Noor is a Bangladeshi-American YouTuber, entrepreneur, and self-love advocate who's built a brand around celebrating diversity, body positivity, and inner beauty. But her journey wasn't a straight shot to success. She faced countless rejections, struggled with self-doubt, and had to navigate the challenges of being a woman of color in a predominantly white beauty industry.

What She Wants You to Know:

- **It's Not Always Smooth Sailing:** "There were times I felt like giving up because I didn't see myself represented, and I didn't feel like I belonged. But those moments taught me to create my own space instead of waiting for someone else to give it to me."
- **Embrace Your Unique Story:** "Your story, your background, and your perspective are what make you stand out. Don't hide the parts of you that are different—those are your superpowers."

Key Takeaway: Success is rarely a straight line. There will be detours, setbacks, and moments of doubt. Embrace your unique path, and remember that every challenge is shaping you into the creator you're meant to be.

THE CONTENT TO CASH BIBLE

2. "It's a Marathon, Not a Sprint." – Ali Abdaal

Ali Abdaal is a former doctor turned YouTuber, entrepreneur, and productivity expert who's known for his in-depth videos on studying, personal development, and building a meaningful life. Ali's channel took years to gain traction, and he's quick to remind new creators that overnight success is often anything but.

What He Wants You to Know:

- **Consistency Beats Perfection:** "When I started my channel, my videos weren't great. I didn't have fancy equipment, and I was awkward on camera. But I kept showing up, kept learning, and kept improving. Consistency is more important than being perfect from day one."
- **Focus on the Process, Not the Results:** "It's easy to get caught up in metrics—views, subscribers, revenue. But what keeps you going is enjoying the process. If you're only chasing numbers, you'll burn out. Find joy in the act of creating."

Key Takeaway: Success doesn't happen overnight, and that's okay. Focus on showing up consistently, enjoying the journey, and celebrating small wins along the way.

3. "You're Not Alone in This." – Matt D'Avella

Matt D'Avella is a filmmaker, YouTuber, and podcast host known for his minimalist approach to life and his beautifully crafted videos on intentional living. Matt's journey was far from glamorous; he spent years working odd jobs and struggling to make ends meet before his YouTube channel took off.

What He Wants You to Know:

- **It's Okay to Struggle:** "There were times when I felt like a complete failure. I was working long hours, barely making rent, and constantly questioning if I was on the right path. But those struggles were part of the process, and they pushed me to keep going."
- **Lean on Your Community:** "Being a creator can feel isolating, but you're not alone. Connect with other creators, share your challenges, and lift each other up. The journey is a lot easier when you have people cheering you on."

Key Takeaway: The struggles you face are not unique, and you're not alone. Lean into your community, be honest about the hard parts, and keep moving forward. The tough times make the victories even sweeter.

Wrapping It All Up: Your Success Story Starts Now

The stories we've shared in this chapter are proof that there's no one-size-fits-all path to success in the creator economy. Every creator's journey is different, shaped by unique challenges, opportunities, and decisions. But the common thread is resilience, passion, and a willingness to keep going when things get tough.

You don't have to be perfect. You don't have to have it all figured out. You just need to start, stay true to your vision, and keep showing up—even when it's hard. The creators you look up to were once where you are now: unsure, hustling, and hoping that their efforts would pay off.

So take these lessons, use these stories as fuel, and keep pushing forward. Your success story is already in the making, and it's going to be incredible.

Let's go make some magic.

CONCLUSION

TURNING YOUR PASSION INTO PROSPERITY

Alright, creators, we've come a long way together in this journey through the creator economy. From finding your niche and building your brand to monetizing your influence and sustaining long-term growth, you now have the tools and insights to take your passion and turn it into something truly powerful. But before we wrap things up, let's take a moment to reflect on what it really takes to win in this game, why you've got everything you need to succeed, and where you can go from here.

This isn't just the end of a book—it's the beginning of your next chapter. So let's dive into the final words of wisdom, encouragement, and some practical resources to keep you moving forward.

Recap of Key Points: What It Takes to Win in the Creator Economy

Winning in the creator economy isn't about luck. It's about strategy, mindset, and the willingness to keep showing up, even when things get tough. Here's a quick recap of the key points we've covered that will set you up for success.

1. Find Your Niche and Own It

The first step in your journey is finding your niche—what makes you unique, what you're passionate about, and how you can provide value. We talked about the importance of identifying your unique voice and honing in on a specific area where you can stand out. The creators who win are those who aren't afraid to be specific, to lean into their weirdness, and to build a brand that's unmistakably theirs.

Key Takeaway: Don't try to be everything to everyone. The more specific you are, the more you'll attract the right audience who truly resonates with you. Embrace your unique voice, and don't be afraid to take up space in your niche.

2. Build a Brand That's Authentic and Consistent

Your brand is more than just your logo or your color scheme—it's your story, your values, and how you connect with your audience. We explored the art of storytelling, the importance of consistency, and how showing up as your true self is the best way to build a loyal community.

Key Takeaway: Consistency builds trust, and authenticity builds connection. Show up as yourself, share your journey—flaws and all—and stay consistent with your message. That's how you create a brand people want to follow.

3. Create Engaging Content That Adds Value

Content is the backbone of the creator economy. But it's not just about pumping out posts—it's about creating content that engages, educates, entertains, and inspires. We talked about content creation strategies, storytelling techniques, and the power of leveraging AI and smart technology to elevate your content game.

Key Takeaway: Focus on quality over quantity. Create content that adds real value to your audience's lives, whether it's through laughter, learning, or inspiration. And don't be afraid to experiment with new formats and tools to keep things fresh.

4. Grow Your Audience with Intentional Engagement

Building an audience isn't just about gaining followers—it's about creating a community. We covered the importance of engaging with your audience, optimizing your social media presence, and using data to refine your approach. Growing your audience requires intentionality, strategy, and a genuine desire to connect with the people who support you.

Key Takeaway: Treat your audience like the valuable community they are. Engage with them, listen to their feedback, and make them feel seen and appreciated. When you build a strong relationship with your audience, they'll stick with you for the long haul.

5. Monetize Your Influence Strategically

Monetizing your influence is where creativity meets entrepreneurship. From sponsored content and affiliate marketing to product sales and courses, we explored multiple ways to turn your influence into income. But monetization isn't just about making money—it's about aligning your revenue streams with your brand values and audience needs.

Key Takeaway: Diversify your income streams and always think long-term. Don't just chase the next payday; build revenue streams that align with your brand and provide real value to your audience. And remember, knowing your worth is key—don't undersell yourself.

6. Manage Your Finances Like a Boss

The financial side of being a creator can be daunting, but it's crucial for your long-term success. We dived into budgeting basics, building a money mindset, and investing for the future. Managing your finances well isn't just about avoiding stress; it's about setting yourself up for a secure and prosperous future.

Key Takeaway: Treat your finances with the respect they deserve. Budget wisely, invest early, and create a financial plan that supports your goals. Your financial health is just as important as your follower count—don't neglect it.

7. Protect Your Legacy with Life Insurance and Financial Security

Life insurance might not be the first thing you think about when building your brand, but it's an essential part of protecting your income, your loved ones, and your legacy. We talked about understanding your life insurance options, choosing the right policy, and planning for the unexpected.

Key Takeaway: Don't overlook the importance of financial security. Life is unpredictable, and having a plan in place ensures that your hard work doesn't go to waste. Protect what you're building—both for yourself and the people you care about.

8. Sustain Long-term Growth with Resilience and Adaptability

Growth isn't just about numbers; it's about staying relevant, evolving with the times, and avoiding burnout. We explored strategies for sustaining long-term growth, from expanding beyond social media to diversifying your income streams and taking care of your mental health.

Key Takeaway: Growth is a marathon, not a sprint. Stay adaptable, keep learning, and prioritize your well-being. The creator economy is constantly changing, and the creators who thrive are the ones who embrace change and keep pushing forward.

9. Learn from Success Stories and Case Studies

Finally, we looked at real-life examples of creators who've made it big, learning from their wins and their mistakes. Their journeys are filled with lessons, best practices, and inspiration that you can apply to your own path.

Key Takeaway: Success leaves clues. Study the creators you admire, learn from their stories, and use their insights as motivation. Remember that every successful creator started somewhere—and your journey is just as valid and full of potential.

Encouragement for Future Creators: You've Got What It Takes

If there's one thing I want you to take away from this book, it's this: You've got what it takes. The creator economy is an incredible opportunity, but it's not always easy. There will be days when the likes aren't coming, the views are low, or the brand deals are scarce. There will be moments of self-doubt, comparison, and questioning whether you're cut out for this.

But here's the truth: Every creator who's ever made it felt those same doubts. They've faced setbacks, heard "no" more times than they can count, and wanted to quit at some point. But they kept going, kept learning, and kept creating. And you can, too.

1. Remember Why You Started

When things get tough, go back to your "why." Why did you start creating in the first place? What lights you up about sharing your voice, your art, or your knowledge with the world? Let that passion drive you forward, even when the external validation isn't there. Your why is your anchor, and it will keep you grounded no matter what.

2. Celebrate Every Win—Big or Small

Success isn't just about the big milestones; it's about the small wins along the way. Did you get your first 100 followers? Celebrate it. Did someone comment that your content made their day? Celebrate that, too. Every step forward is worth acknowledging, and those small wins add up to big progress over time.

3. Be Patient with Your Journey

It's easy to look at other creators and feel like you're falling behind. But success isn't a race, and everyone's timeline is different. Be patient with your journey and trust that your hard work will pay off in its own time. You're exactly where you need to be right now— keep moving forward, one step at a time.

4. Embrace Failure as Part of the Process

Failure isn't the opposite of success; it's a part of it. Every misstep, every rejection, and every flop is a learning opportunity. Instead of letting failure discourage you, let it be a stepping stone. The creators who win are the ones who keep getting back up, no matter how many times they fall.

5. You Are More Capable Than You Think

Self-doubt is a sneaky beast, but here's the thing—you are more capable, talented, and resourceful than you give yourself credit for. You've already made it this far, and you've got the skills, the passion, and the drive to keep going. Don't let the fear of not being enough hold you back. You are enough, just as you are.

Resources and Tools for Continued Growth: Where to Go from Here

As you continue on your journey, here are some resources and tools that can help you keep learning, growing, and thriving in the creator economy.

1. Online Learning Platforms: Keep Expanding Your Skills

- **Skillshare:** Perfect for creators looking to learn new skills in areas like graphic design, video editing, marketing, and more. Courses are taught by industry professionals and can be done at your own pace.

- **MasterClass:** Learn from the best in the business, from famous chefs and artists to filmmakers and entrepreneurs. MasterClass offers high-quality video lessons that can inspire and educate you in your craft.
- **Udemy:** With thousands of courses on practically every topic under the sun, Udemy is a great platform to deepen your knowledge or pick up new skills that can enhance your brand.

2. Tools for Content Creation and Management

1. **Canva:** An easy-to-use design tool for creating everything from social media graphics to e-book covers. Canva's templates make it accessible even if you're not a graphic designer.
2. **Final Cut Pro / Adobe Premiere Pro:** For creators serious about video content, these are industry-standard tools for editing high-quality videos. They offer advanced features that will take your video content to the next level.
3. **Notion / Trello / Asana:** Project management tools that help you keep track of content ideas, deadlines, and workflows. Staying organized is key to staying consistent.

3. Platforms for Building Your Owned Audience

- **ConvertKit:** A popular email marketing platform for creators. ConvertKit allows you to grow your email list, create automated sequences, and connect directly with your audience.

- **Substack:** A great option if you want to start a newsletter and monetize your writing. Substack allows you to build a subscriber base and offer both free and paid content.
- **Mighty Networks:** If you're looking to build a community off social media, Mighty Networks offers a platform to create your own branded community space with courses, groups, and more.

4. Financial Tools for Creators

- **QuickBooks / FreshBooks:** Accounting software designed for freelancers and small business owners. These tools help you keep track of your income, expenses, and taxes, making financial management easier.
- **Mint:** A free budgeting app that allows you to track your spending, set savings goals, and manage your finances all in one place.
- **Robinhood / Vanguard:** If you're ready to start investing, these platforms make it easy to buy stocks, ETFs, and more. Investing is a great way to build long-term wealth alongside your creator income.

5. Mental Health and Wellness Resources

- **Headspace / Calm:** Meditation apps that help you manage stress, anxiety, and burnout. Taking care of your mental health is crucial, and these apps offer guided meditations, sleep sounds, and mindfulness exercises.

- **BetterHelp:** An online therapy platform that connects you with licensed therapists from the comfort of your home. If you're feeling overwhelmed, talking to a professional can provide valuable support.
- **Fitness Apps (Peloton, FitOn, MyFitnessPal):** Staying active and taking care of your physical health can do wonders for your mental well-being. Fitness apps provide workouts, meal plans, and motivation to keep you moving.

Your Journey Is Just Beginning

So here we are, at the end of this book but the start of something much bigger. The creator economy is full of opportunities, and you have everything it takes to seize them. You've got the passion, the knowledge, and the drive. Now, it's time to go out there and make your mark.

Remember, every big success story started with a first step, and every creator you admire was once a beginner, just like you. Don't let fear or self-doubt hold you back from chasing your dreams. You've got the tools, the insights, and the heart to build something amazing.

So keep creating, keep learning, and keep pushing forward. The world needs your voice, your art, and your unique perspective. Your journey in the creator economy is just getting started, and I can't wait to see where it takes you.

You've got this. Now go out there and show the world what you're made of.

APPENDICES

YOUR TOOLKIT FOR THRIVING IN THE CREATOR ECONOMY

C ongratulations on making it to the Appendices! If you've read this far, you're serious about leveling up in the creator economy, and you're ready to dive even deeper. The journey doesn't end with this book—it's just the beginning. In this section, we're going to equip you with a toolkit of resources, terms, and further reading that will keep you growing, learning, and thriving.

Whether you're just starting out or you've been in the game for a while, having the right resources can make all the difference. From essential apps and websites to key terms you need to know and books that will inspire and educate you, this is your go-to guide for continued success. Let's get into it.

Additional Resources and Tools: Apps, Websites, and Communities

In the creator economy, having the right tools at your disposal can streamline your workflow, boost your productivity, and elevate the quality of your content. Below is a curated list of apps, websites, and communities that every creator should know about.

1. Content Creation and Design Tools

- **Canva:** This is a must-have for any creator looking to design social media graphics, presentations, e-books, or any other visual content. Canva's user-friendly interface and countless templates make it accessible for everyone, from design novices to pros.
- **Adobe Creative Cloud (Photoshop, Illustrator, Premiere Pro):** For creators looking to take their design and editing skills to the next level, Adobe Creative Cloud is the industry standard. Photoshop and Illustrator are perfect for graphic design, while Premiere Pro is a go-to for video editing.
- **Final Cut Pro:** If you're into video creation and want an alternative to Adobe, Final Cut Pro is a powerful video editing software used by many YouTubers and filmmakers. It's great for Mac users and offers a more intuitive interface compared to other editing tools.
- **Procreate:** For artists and illustrators, Procreate is a top-tier digital illustration app available on iPad. It's perfect

for creating custom artwork, digital products, and social media graphics on the go.

- **Descript:** A game-changer for podcasters and video creators, Descript allows you to edit audio and video by editing the transcript. It's fast, intuitive, and saves a ton of time, especially when working with interviews or long-form content.

2. Social Media Management and Analytics

- **Buffer / Hootsuite:** These platforms help you schedule and manage your social media posts across multiple channels. They're perfect for keeping your content consistent and engaging without having to be online 24/7.

- **Later:** Specifically designed for Instagram, Later allows you to plan and schedule your posts with a visual drag-and-drop calendar. It's a great way to maintain a cohesive Instagram aesthetic and keep your content on track.

- **Sprout Social:** For those looking for more in-depth social media analytics, Sprout Social offers powerful insights into your audience's behavior, engagement, and growth trends. It's a bit pricier but worth it if you're serious about data-driven social strategy.

- **Google Analytics:** Understanding your website traffic is crucial if you have a blog, online store, or any web presence. Google Analytics provides detailed reports on your site visitors, showing you what's working and what's not.

- **Social Blade:** Want to see how your growth stacks up against other creators? Social Blade provides analytics for YouTube, Instagram, TikTok, and Twitch, offering insights into follower counts, engagement rates, and channel growth.

3. Financial Tools and Resources

- **QuickBooks / FreshBooks:** Managing your finances as a creator can be a headache, but these accounting tools make it easier. They help you track income, expenses, and taxes, keeping your business finances organized and stress-free.

- **Wave:** For creators just starting out, Wave offers free invoicing, accounting, and receipt scanning software. It's a great tool to keep your finances in check without the upfront costs.

- **Robinhood / Vanguard / Fidelity:** Investing is a great way to grow your wealth alongside your creator income. These platforms make it easy to buy stocks, ETFs, and more. Robinhood is user-friendly for beginners, while Vanguard and Fidelity offer more robust investment options.

- **You Need A Budget (YNAB):** If budgeting is a struggle, YNAB is here to help. This app guides you to allocate every dollar with purpose, helping you save more, spend wisely, and get ahead of your expenses.

4. Productivity and Project Management

- **Notion:** Notion is a one-stop shop for note-taking, project management, and personal organization. It's perfect for keeping track of content ideas, managing to-do lists, and collaborating with your team—all in one place.
- **Trello:** Trello's board system makes it easy to visualize your workflow and keep projects moving. Use it to plan your content calendar, manage tasks, or collaborate on bigger projects.
- **Asana:** Another great tool for project management, Asana helps you track your tasks, deadlines, and progress. It's especially useful if you're managing a team or juggling multiple projects at once.
- **Evernote:** For those who love jotting down ideas on the go, Evernote is an excellent note-taking app that syncs across all your devices. Keep all your creative inspirations, notes, and research organized in one easy-to-access place.

5. Communities and Networking

- **Creator Economy Expo (CEX):** A must-attend event for creators looking to connect, learn, and grow. CEX brings together creators, entrepreneurs, and influencers to share insights on building sustainable creator businesses.
- **Patreon Community:** More than just a platform for monetization, Patreon offers a community where creators

share tips, resources, and support one another in growing their membership platforms.

- **The Rising Tide Society:** A community for creative entrepreneurs and small business owners. Their motto, "community over competition," fosters a supportive environment where creators can share advice, collaborate, and grow together.

- **Reddit (r/CreatorServices, r/Entrepreneur, r/Small-Business):** Reddit can be a goldmine for creators looking to network, get advice, or troubleshoot issues. There are countless subreddits dedicated to creators and entrepreneurs sharing their experiences and tips.

Glossary of Terms: Understanding the Lingo of the Creator Economy

Navigating the creator economy means getting familiar with its unique language. Whether you're new to the scene or just need a refresher, here's a glossary of key terms that every creator should know.

Affiliate Marketing: A type of marketing where creators earn a commission for promoting a company's products or services. When someone makes a purchase through the creator's unique affiliate link, the creator earns a percentage of the sale.

Algorithm: The system used by social media platforms to determine what content is shown to users. Algorithms consider factors like engagement, relevance, and user behavior to prioritize content in feeds.

Analytics: Data and metrics that provide insights into the performance of your content. This includes views, clicks, likes, shares, and more. Understanding your analytics helps you refine your strategy and grow your audience.

Call to Action (CTA): A prompt that encourages your audience to take a specific action, like subscribing to your channel, following your social media, or purchasing a product. CTAs are crucial for driving engagement and conversions.

Click-Through Rate (CTR): The percentage of people who click on a link, ad, or call to action compared to the number of people who see it. A high CTR indicates effective, engaging content.

Collab (Collaboration): A partnership between two or more creators or brands to produce content together. Collabs can help expand your reach, introduce you to new audiences, and create valuable networking opportunities.

Content Calendar: A schedule that outlines what content you plan to publish and when. A content calendar helps you stay organized, maintain consistency, and plan ahead for holidays, launches, or themed content.

Content Pillars: Key themes or topics that your content revolves around. Identifying your content pillars helps ensure that your posts are aligned with your brand and provide value to your audience.

Creator Fund: A program set up by platforms like TikTok and YouTube to pay creators based on the performance of their content. Funds are typically calculated based on views, engagement, and other factors.

Engagement Rate: A metric that measures the amount of interaction (likes, comments, shares) your content receives compared to your total number of followers. A high engagement rate indicates strong audience interest and connection.

Evergreen Content: Content that remains relevant and valuable over time, rather than being tied to current events or trends. Examples include how-to guides, tutorials, and timeless advice that continues to attract views long after it's published.

Funnel (Sales Funnel): A marketing model that illustrates the journey a customer takes from first discovering your brand to making a purchase. Funnels often include stages like awareness, consideration, and conversion.

Impressions: The number of times your content is displayed to users, regardless of whether it's clicked. Impressions help gauge the visibility of your content but don't necessarily reflect engagement.

Influencer Marketing: A strategy where brands partner with creators to promote their products or services to the creator's audience. Influencers leverage their trust and authority to encourage their followers to take action.

Key Performance Indicators (KPIs): Metrics used to measure the success of your content or strategy. Common KPIs for creators include engagement rate, follower growth, and revenue generated from brand partnerships. Tracking your KPIs helps you understand what's working and where you need to adjust your efforts.

Livestreaming: Broadcasting live video content to your audience in real-time. Platforms like Instagram, YouTube, and Twitch offer livestreaming capabilities, allowing creators to connect with their followers, answer questions, and provide behind-the-scenes access.

Media Kit: A document that creators use to present their brand to potential partners, showcasing their audience demographics, engagement rates, past collaborations, and services offered. A well-designed media kit is essential for negotiating brand deals.

Monetization: The process of earning money from your content. This can include ad revenue, sponsorships, merchandise sales, membership platforms like Patreon, and more. Monetization is key to turning your creative passion into a sustainable business.

Niche: A specific segment of the market that you focus your content on. Your niche helps define your target audience and differentiate you from other creators. A well-defined niche can lead to a more engaged and loyal following.

Organic Reach: The number of people who see your content without paid promotion. Organic reach is influenced by how often your followers engage with your content, as well as the algorithms of the platforms you're using.

Pitch: A proposal or presentation to a potential brand partner, sponsor, or collaborator outlining why they should work with you. A strong pitch highlights your unique value, audience, and the benefits of partnering with your brand.

Repurposing Content: The practice of taking a piece of content and adapting it for different platforms or formats. For example, turning a YouTube video into an Instagram reel, a blog post, or a podcast episode. Repurposing extends the life of your content and maximizes its reach.

ROI (Return on Investment): A measure of the profitability of an investment. In the context of the creator economy, ROI might refer to the success of an ad campaign, the impact of a new content strategy, or the financial return from a business expense.

Sponsorship: A partnership where a brand pays a creator to promote their product or service in content. Sponsorships are one of the most common ways creators monetize their platforms and are often negotiated based on reach, engagement, and audience fit.

Subscriber-Only Content: Exclusive content that's only accessible to subscribers or paying members. This can include Patreon perks, YouTube channel memberships, or premium newsletter content. Offering subscriber-only content can build a dedicated fanbase and create an additional revenue stream.

Thumbnails: The cover images that represent your video content on platforms like YouTube. A good thumbnail grabs attention and entices viewers to click, making it one of the most important elements for driving video views.

UGC (User-Generated Content): Content created by your audience that features your brand, product, or service. UGC can include customer reviews, tagged posts, and fan-created content. It's a powerful way to build community and social proof.

Virality: The phenomenon where content rapidly spreads across the internet, gaining massive exposure in a short period of time. While virality is often unpredictable, creating highly shareable, relatable, or shocking content can increase your chances of going viral.

Recommended Reading and References: Books and Articles to Deepen Your Knowledge

Books, articles, and other resources are invaluable for creators who want to keep growing and learning. Whether you're looking for inspiration, business advice, or deeper insights into the creator economy, the following list will help you take your knowledge to the next level.

1. Books for Creators

- **"YouTube Secrets" by Sean Cannell and Benji Travis:** This is a must-read for anyone serious about building a YouTube channel. Sean and Benji dive into the strategies that successful creators use to grow their channels, monetize their content, and build an audience.

- **"Show Your Work!" by Austin Kleon:** A fantastic guide for creators who want to build an audience by sharing their creative process. Austin Kleon's insights are practical, encouraging, and perfect for anyone who struggles with putting their work out there.

- **"Crushing It!" by Gary Vaynerchuk:** In this book, Gary Vee shares real-life stories of creators who have built successful personal brands and businesses using social media. It's filled with practical advice, inspiration, and a no-nonsense approach to getting started.

- **"The War of Art" by Steven Pressfield:** This book tackles the mental battles that every creator faces—procrastination, self-doubt, and fear of failure. Pressfield's insights will help you push past the resistance and stay committed to your creative path.

- **"Contagious: How to Build Word of Mouth in the Digital Age" by Jonah Berger:** If you want to understand why content goes viral, this book is for you. Berger breaks down the science behind what makes people share and how you can apply those principles to your own content.

- **"Big Magic: Creative Living Beyond Fear" by Elizabeth Gilbert:** This is a great read for creators struggling with perfectionism or fear of failure. Gilbert's wisdom on the creative process and her encouragement to live a more creative life will resonate deeply with any creator.

- **"The Lean Startup" by Eric Ries:** For creators looking to build a business or launch a new product, this book offers a framework for testing ideas, learning quickly, and scaling sustainably. It's a go-to for anyone wanting to approach their creative career like a startup.

- **"Building a StoryBrand" by Donald Miller:** This book is all about clarifying your message and crafting a compelling brand narrative. It's especially useful for creators who want to connect more deeply with their audience and stand out in a crowded market.

- **"Abundance Is Your Birthright: The 9 True Spiritual Beliefs That Will Make You a Millionaire! (And the 9 False Beliefs That Have Kept You Broke)" by Ash Cash:** This powerful book helps faith-based individuals access the wealth promised to them by God. Drawing from ancient spiritual texts like the Bible, the Quran, and the Torah, as well as Universal Laws such as the Law of Attraction, Ash Cash provides a roadmap to unlocking your abundance. By understanding the science of getting rich through spiritual beliefs, this book empowers you to claim the financial freedom that is your birthright.

2. Articles and Blogs

- **"The Creator Economy Explained" by SignalFire:** A comprehensive breakdown of the creator economy, including key trends, data, and predictions for the future. This article is perfect for understanding the broader landscape and where you fit in.
- **"Why TikTok Stars Are Leaving Major Social Media Platforms" by The Verge:** An insightful look into the evolving dynamics of the creator economy, including why some creators are shifting away from traditional social media platforms in favor of direct monetization.
- **"The State of the Creator Economy" by The Influencer Marketing Hub:** This annual report dives into the latest data on influencer marketing, creator income, and the changing landscape. It's an essential read to keep up with current trends.
- **"Patreon's Role in the Creator Economy" by Fast Company:** This article explores how platforms like Patreon are revolutionizing the way creators earn income and build communities. It's a great read for anyone considering launching a membership model.
- **"How to Make a Media Kit for Brand Partnerships" by Later:** A practical guide to creating a media kit that gets noticed by brands. This article includes tips,

examples, and templates to help you present your best self to potential partners.

- **"Understanding YouTube's Algorithm" by TubeFilter:** A detailed explanation of how YouTube's algorithm works and what creators can do to optimize their content for maximum reach. A must-read for anyone serious about growing on YouTube.

3. Podcasts and YouTube Channels

- **"The Tim Ferriss Show" (Podcast):** Tim Ferriss interviews world-class performers from different fields, unpacking their routines, strategies, and tools for success. It's full of actionable insights for creators who want to level up.
- **"GaryVee Audio Experience" (Podcast):** Gary Vaynerchuk shares no-BS advice on entrepreneurship, social media, and building a personal brand. It's a mix of keynote speeches, interviews, and fireside chats that are perfect for creators at any stage.
- **"Inside the Vault with Ash Cash" (Podcast):** Ash Cash dives into wealth-building strategies, financial literacy, and entrepreneurial success, blending hip-hop culture with practical advice. A great resource for creators looking to understand the business side of things.
- **"Creative Pep Talk" (Podcast):** Hosted by Andy J. Pizza, this podcast is all about helping creators break through creative blocks and find their unique voice. It's

packed with inspiration, practical tips, and encouragement to keep pushing forward.

- **"Ali Abdaal" (YouTube Channel):** Ali Abdaal shares insights on productivity, personal development, and building a meaningful life as a creator. His videos are both motivational and practical, making complex topics feel accessible.
- **"Think Media" (YouTube Channel):** A fantastic resource for creators looking to improve their video quality, grow their YouTube channel, and learn the ins and outs of content creation. Think Media offers tutorials, gear reviews, and marketing tips.

Your Resource Library: Keep Learning, Keep Growing

As a creator, your education doesn't end—it's an ongoing process of learning, adapting, and evolving. The resources listed here are just the tip of the iceberg, and as the creator economy continues to grow, so will the tools and opportunities available to you. Bookmark the ones that resonate, dive into the ones that challenge you, and keep pushing yourself to explore new ideas.

Remember, the creator economy is constantly evolving, and the most successful creators are the ones who stay curious, keep learning, and aren't afraid to experiment. So take what you've learned, apply it, and continue building your path forward.

The journey is just beginning, and the possibilities are endless. Keep creating, keep growing, and keep showing the world what you're made of.

www.ingramcontent.com/pod-product-compliance
Lightning Source LLC
Chambersburg PA
CBHW071604210326
41597CB00019B/3390